CW01207095

THE WALDEN INTERVIEWS

edited by

DAVID COX

LWT

Boxtree

First published in 1990 by Boxtree Limited

The Walden Interviews copyright © London Weekend Television 1990
Foreword and Introductions copyright © David Cox 1990
Front jacket photograph: Topham
Back jacket photograph: London Weekend Television

British Library Cataloguing in Publication Data
The Walden Interviews.
1. Great Britain. Politics
I. Cox, David
320.941

ISBN 1-85283-104-9

Edited by Janita Clamp & Christopher Walker
Designed by Julia Lilauwala
Typeset by Action Typesetting Ltd
Printed and bound in the UK by Richard Clay Ltd
for Boxtree Ltd, 36 Tavistock Street, London WC2E 7PB.

CONTENTS

FOREWORD

Last autumn, as in previous periods of political excitement, I was asked if I wished I was back in the Commons. This time I was also asked something else. Now that the proceedings of the House were being televised, hadn't my present occupation become redundant? Why should politicians need to be questioned by broadcasters when we can watch them being put through their paces by their peers?

My response to each of these questions was the same. Much as I respect the House of Commons, and fond though my memories are of my 13 years at Westminster, I am in no doubt that Parliament is an incomplete guarantor of our liberties, even when it is televised. I am equally certain that the televised political interview can add something of real value to the activities of our Parliamentarians. Anyone who doubts this should read the text of Mrs Thatcher's interview on Nigel Lawson's resignation in this book and then compare it with *Hansard*'s account of her responses to Neil Kinnock at Prime Minister's Questions on the following Tuesday. The interview does not clear up all the outstanding issues, but it undoubtedly sheds light on some of them. The same cannot be said for the Parliamentary answers, in which Mrs Thatcher easily avoids giving any meaningful response. This is not Mr Kinnock's fault. The plain fact is that Westminster's time-honoured procedures for calling our leaders to account are in some respects vastly inferior to those of television, hard though this is to accept for those who still resent the medium's sometimes malign command over societies like our own.

As has long been recognised in our judicial system, when it comes to uncovering truth there is no substitute for sustained questioning in public by a single individual armed with a clear purpose. Parliamentary questions, debates, speeches, press conferences and long newspaper articles may all have their place. But they are not enough.

We should be proud that we in Britain have made the political interview a more effective instrument of liberty than any of the other peoples of the democratic world. You will not find interviews like those recorded in this book on the television screens of the United States, where communication between leaders and led is stuck at the stage of the Presidential fireside chat and the stilted, televised press conference. Nor will you find the presidents and chancellors of democracies as apparently similar to our own as those of France or West Germany participating in the kind of exchanges which we take for granted on British television. That our own politicians speak as directly as they do to interviewers doubtless has something to do with our tradition of robust public argument and the peculiar intimacy of our political culture. But it also says something for our politicians.

Politicians are usually represented as liars, cheats and charlatans. There is some truth in this stereotype, as in so many others, and our scepticism about the motives of those who wish to boss us about is one of the healthier of our national characteristics. Nonetheless, now that I have matched my 13 years at Westminster with another 13 in the TV interviewer's chair, I have to report that what I have encountered there has not been all bad. I have heard many lies, much prevarication and a great deal of unwelcome obfuscation. But I have also heard, far more often than I expected to, straight talk about serious matters. More than once I have met with honesty so impolitic that it has cost my interviewee his job. If I have interviewed the wilfully dishonest, I have also interviewed decent people with things of value to say. Though I have tried to expose the deceptions of the former, I have considered it no less important a task to scrutinise the ideas of the latter.

It is because I am convinced that the work I have come to do matters, that I view the future with foreboding. There are those who tell me that the political interview is the one form of current affairs programming which is bound to survive the increased financial pressure on the television industry which more competition will bring. After all, interviewing is, they tell me, dirt cheap and dead easy.

It is indeed easy to stick a politician in a chair and ask him a few questions. Unfortunately, the result will not necessarily constitute a serious political interview. There may be people who can conduct proper interviews with little effort and no aid. But I doubt it. Certainly I cannot. My performance each Sunday reflects the dedicated effort of a team of highly trained, talented, experienced and therefore expensive people working over a period of weeks, as you will appreciate if you read David Cox's introduction. During my years with London Weekend Television, the necessity for this effort has always been understood and it has always been provided. However, as the broadcasting environment changes, it is far from clear that serious political interviewing will continue to command either sufficient resources or sufficient air-time, even at Sunday lunch-time, on the commercial channels.

If political interviewing withers on the commercial channels, we cannot assume it will be safe in the hands of the BBC. Up till now it has been competition between ITV and the BBC which has maintained standards. If that competition fades, I fear for my craft.

The interviews in this book are being published because it was felt that they illuminated aspects of politics which will remain important over what look like being the eventful years ahead. I shall certainly use this book myself as essential background material when preparing future interviews. I hope it will help you too. If it does, I trust you will come to agree with me that political interviewing matters and that it ought to continue to play its part in our national life. If enough of us want it to, we can ensure that it will. For though it has suited some to pretend otherwise, broadcasting, as much as anything else, is subject to the democratic process of which the political interview is a part.

BRIAN WALDEN, *May, 1990*

INTRODUCTION

The autumn of 1989 saw British politics wake abruptly from a state of torpor which some had considered terminal. Hard though it is to believe it now, after Mrs Thatcher's third election victory in 1987 there were those who argued that the era of political struggle in Britain had come to an end. Was not the message of the 1980s that decision-making could and should be shifted from the citizen to the consumer, that age-old conflicts had given way to the common pursuit of material enrichment and that the scope for public policy-making must therefore shrink? It was amid such murmurings that Britain was suddenly beset by economic crisis in all too familiar a form, the collapse of the post-war order in Europe and the new trauma of environmental degradation. At the same time, the Labour Party re-emerged as a serious contender for power and Mrs Thatcher, who had single-handedly set the agenda for the decade, showed the first real signs of losing her hitherto certain touch. It was a good time for political interviewing. But not for the political interview.

The sorry state of this once respected instrument of democratic dialogue had become a dinner-table discussion topic for the chattering classes. It seemed a long time since anything very significant or memorable had happened in a television interview, and people were wondering what had gone wrong. In *The Spectator*, Paul Johnson asked "if the set-piece television interview is dying", and both *The Media Show* and *The Late Show* ran items lamenting the apparent ineffectiveness of political interviewing on television.

No less a figure than Sir Robin Day, who could justly claim to have invented the political interview, was on hand with a diagnosis. The patient had not, as optimists might have supposed, succumbed to a passing malaise; it had actually expired. In his autobiography, *Grand Inquisitor*, Sir Robin laid the blame for this regrettable state of affairs on two politicians – Margaret Thatcher and, to a lesser extent, Neil Kinnock. By treating interviewers' questions "as tiresome interruptions to the impressive flow of Thatcherite statistics or Kinnockian rhetoric" they had turned interviews into "a series of statements, planned for delivery irrespective of the question which had been put". As a result, the political interview had been "hijacked by the politicians" and was now "rarely a dialogue which could be helpful to the viewer".

Sir Robin's was not the only explanation put forward for the decline of the political interview. Conspiracy-minded journalists preferred the idea that politicians had taken to requiring producers to agree in advance that difficult questions would not be asked, as the price for participating in programmes. Either way, the message seemed to be clear: the political interview was dead because politicians had found ways of emasculating the interviewer. It was a message which fitted the mood of a time when broadcasters generally were thought to have been cowed by the Thatcher government's many-fronted onslaught against them.

This, then, was the background – politically auspicious but professionally clouded – against which *The Walden Interview* took to the screen in September 1989. The programme had been conceived the previous year as a short-term stop-gap. But if its origins were humble, it was not without potential.

The most obvious of the programme's assets was its eponymous interviewer. Brian Walden spent 13 years in the House of Commons. Because of this, politicians tend to feel that they cannot fob him off with a piece of guff which might suffice elsewhere. Moreover, though Walden may be a diminutive figure cursed with both a speech impediment and one of the weirdest accents to which the air-waves have ever played host, he is thought to have magic powers. Is it true, a faintly anxious politician may ask before an interview, that Walden can name from memory the players in every First and Second Division side this century and can quote the exact result recorded in every state at every Presidential election in the history of the USA? (It is.)

It might be thought that somebody of Walden's exalted standing, switching jobs in mid-life, would have considered such advantages quite enough to get him by. But Walden did not. He decided that if he was to succeed in his new career, a lot of work would have to get done and that he was prepared to do it, even though one of his attributes in legend, if not in fact, is idleness so all-consuming that it requires him to take to his bed for weeks at a time. He became convinced however that his own work would not be enough. Some performers try to do everything themselves and restrict their production staff to running errands. The price they pay is that their performance can only be as good as their own talents in all areas will allow, and these may not be enough. Walden decided that if he was to maximise his potential he must not depend on his own talents, however considerable others might believe them to be. He is convinced that his experience and temperament make him well fitted to conduct political interviews, but he believes that planning them is better left to others. This makes him very dependent on the calibre of his team, and on this front *The Walden Interview* was once more fortunate.

The programme editor, John Wakefield, had learned his trade with Walden on *Weekend World* and knew political interviewing inside out. His two producers were relatively new to television, but they knew about politics: Iain Picton had been Chairman of the Tory Reform Group; Frank Millar had been Chief Executive of Ulster's Official Unionists. Their two researchers, Simon Gornick and Marion Milne, were relatively new to politics, but both were diligent and bright.

Besides its interviewer and its team, *The Walden Interview* had another advantage: its running time. Each week we were to have 43 minutes of normally live and always unedited interview time. There was (and is) no other weekly programme prepared to devote that amount of time to one political interview, and we were determined to make the most of the opportunity. We decided to devote each programme to one subject. There would be no *tours d'horizon*, in which the interviewer would tick off unrelated questions on a clipboard shopping list. If we wanted to know whether Sir Geoffrey Howe would stand up to Mrs Thatcher, our questions would all be aimed at finding that out.

To raise a number of different subjects in a long interview is to turn it into a series of short ones. There are already plenty of short political interviews on British television: usually their purpose is to establish someone's latest policy position, and in these circumstances they work well. But we wanted the scope to pursue other purposes, and some of those would only be successfully achieved through an extended line of questioning. To test Sir Geoffrey's resolve, we first invited him to make statements of intent; but in order to evaluate these statements we also asked him how he proposed to behave in a series of particular situations. The contrast was revealing. If the viewer had been able to rely only on Sir Geoffrey's protestations, he would have been misled.

What, then, were the purposes we were to pursue during these lengthy lunchtime dialogues? Naturally enough we wanted to explore such of the great issues of the day as deserved prolonged examination. These would include both urgent questions of the moment, like those raised by Nigel Lawson's resignation, and questions we ourselves had deemed important, like the seriousness or lack of it of the Government's professed commitment to the environment. Yet trying to enhance the understanding of issues was not to be our only purpose. Politicians deplore attention to "personalities" when it suits them to do so, but in fact it is perfectly sensible. At the 1979 general election we were not to know we were choosing the leader who would have to deal with the invasion of the Falklands, but we could still choose whether we wanted to be led by someone like James Callaghan or someone like Margaret Thatcher. How are we to judge the mettle of our leaders and potential leaders? Political interviews provide us with as good a way as any, almost irrespective of their overt subject matter on any particular occasion. So we wanted *The Walden Interview* to display the character of its participants.

Our style of questioning would be insistent, but we should not hector or belabour, at least as long as the interviewee gave proper answers. Jeremy Paxman of the BBC's *Newsnight* told *The Media Show*'s viewers that interviewers should ask themselves, "Why is this lying bastard lying to me?" We decided to approach the job with the opposite assumption. Suppose this person actually means what he or she is saying. Suppose the viewers might actually be interested. What then? Questioning ought to be able to establish whether the propositions being advanced were internally consistent and whether they conflicted with other things which might matter to viewers. It might establish how committed an interviewee was or how ready to compromise. It might indeed establish that he was lying. We certainly thought our best chance of establishing any of these things lay in taking the whole business as seriously as possible.

The interviewees were going to be serious enough, but their purpose would be different from ours. If our aim was truth, they would be out to win hearts and minds for their causes. Fair enough, if they won them fairly. Yet if that was to happen, our interviewer would have to be not only on top of the facts but also prepared for every possible stratagem and equipped in advance to defeat it.

Once we had settled on a subject and secured the interviewee's agreement to appear, a producer and a researcher would be assigned to assemble information and start drafting questions. They might have weeks; they might have hours. Either way, their work would culminate in the preparation of a document setting out not only the questions to be asked, but all the possible responses we could imagine, together with the follow-ups appropriate for each. At each point where the interviewee had a choice, two completely different lines of questioning would have to be provided, so the whole thing would have the underlying shape of a family-tree. After repeated revisions, this often bulky document would provide the basis for an all-day session on the Friday or the Saturday before the programme. In this meeting we tried to anticipate the likely frame of mind of the interviewee at each stage of the process, and adjusted both our tactics and the phrasing of the questions accordingly. A final version of the questions would then be typed up, and Walden would take it away. In the hours that remained, he would pore over this, pacing about his room, until he had consigned its contents to some deep level of his consciousness. There they would fuse with his own instinctive attitudes and equip him to engage his interviewee without benefit of notes in apparently spontaneous discourse.

This is of course not the only way of doing television interviews, and some other interviewers view the Walden method with horror, disdain or disbelief. How, though, did it stand up in the face of all those diabolical ruses which the politicians were supposed to have in store for the likes of us? What about insistence on restricting the area of questioning as a condition of participation? The fact is that we did not once encounter an attempt by an interviewee or potential interviewee to strike any such deal. We told them what we wanted to ask them about and they told us whether or not they would come. No one even asked for a detailed account of what he or she would be asked. Such apparent insouciance is not necessarily unwise. There are good reasons why an interviewee should not try to pre-empt the asking of obvious questions. At least some viewers will notice, and they cannot be relied upon to blame the interviewer's incompetence. They may suspect that a deal has been struck, and though they may think the less of the programme because of this, they will also be forcefully made aware that the interviewee has something to hide. A politician who decides to open himself to questioning at all is best advised to come equipped with answers, or at least responses, to the questions of the hour.

Mrs Thatcher was as well placed as an interviewee could ever be to try to restrict the questioning when she appeared on *The Walden Interview* on 29 October. When we agreed the terms on which she was to appear on 7 August, we made no mention of any plan to interrogate her about Nigel Lawson's resignation, which was not then in prospect. Had she wanted to, she could have told us when he resigned that she did not want to talk about this subject. She would have known that we might then have withdrawn our invitation, as indeed we should have done, but that would have been the limit of the sanctions available to us. In fact, like all our other interviewees, she seemed to feel she should be expected to deal with whatever Walden chose to throw at her. It is an attitude which might surprise overseas politicians who demand questions in triplicate three weeks before they meet a journalist, but it is doubtless one of the healthier consequences of the British tradition of unscripted Parliamentary confrontation.

Of course, politicians could still refuse to turn up. This right was exercised by Mikhail Gorbachev, F.W. de Klerk (for this series, at least) and (on the grounds that none of the dates offered was suitable) Neil Kinnock. Mieczyslaw Rakowski, the then First Secretary of the then Polish Communist Party, disappeared into a Warsaw clinic with pneumonia the day before his interview was due to take place. But that was pretty much all the obstruction which we encountered outside the studio.

Once an interviewee had turned up, we still had to get him to answer the questions. But even here, in spite of Sir Robin's anxieties, we did not encounter all that much recalcitrance, as you will see from the texts of the interviews. Certainly there was no sign that Mrs Thatcher and Mr Kinnock had so polluted the well of democratic dialogue that it had become impossible to conduct a political interview. Sir Geoffrey Howe and Nigel Lawson both knew that they would pay a price for giving straight answers to the questions they faced, but they both gave them. Bryan Gould chose to incur serious political embarrassment for himself and his party rather than even try to duck an awkward question.

There are still politicians who believe that the smart thing to do in an interview is to ignore the question and to utter instead a speech prepared in advance. Advice to do just this is sometimes doled out to politicians foolish enough to pay for it at expensive courses. The advice, however, is based on the assumption that the viewer is stupid, and this is a rather dangerous assumption to make. Many viewers spend much more time watching television than politicians or, for that matter, producers. They understand its grammar very well, and if they hear a question asked in an interview, they will expect to hear it answered, unless the interviewee can come up with a good reason why it should not be. Today the vast majority of politicians seem to have realised this.

There are nonetheless occasions on which an interviewee will see fit to respond with what masquerades as an answer but is in fact something else. In *The Walden Interview* we encountered this only once in a persistent form, and it will come as no surprise to Sir Robin to learn that the interviewee involved was Margaret Thatcher. During the 1987 election campaign, Peter Bull and Kate Mayer of York University analysed eight interviews given by Mrs Thatcher and Mr Kinnock. They identified eleven main types of evasion, and in her interview with Brian Walden on 29 October 1989 Mrs Thatcher deployed no fewer than ten of them. But does that mean this was not, in Sir Robin's phrase, "a dialogue which could be helpful to the viewer"?

This might be the case if there were no more to a television interview than the extraction of information, but an interview is also a theatrical encounter played out in public. A response which does not constitute an answer can still be extremely productive if the interviewer handles it properly. The rules of procedure in a political interview are as strict and as well understood as those in a criminal trial. They offer protection to the interviewee against bullying, the deployment of false testimony and unnecessary interruption. But they also offer protection to the interviewer. If he deems an interviewee to be providing unsatisfactory answers to reasonable questions, he can say so. If an interviewee suggests, as Mrs Thatcher did, that she is being asked the wrong questions, he can remind her that it is his job not hers to decide what the questions should be.

Disputes between interviewer and interviewee can be referred by either party to higher authority, the audience. Politicians frequently make such appeals, but they are just as readily available to the interviewer. Mrs Thatcher's contention that questions about the Lawson resignation constituted tittle-tattle to which she did not need to reply was only going to work if she could persuade the audience that it was reasonable. Doubtless she did persuade some viewers; but Walden assumed enough viewers would be unpersuaded to make it worthwhile for him to fight on. Mrs Thatcher's demeanour as the interview proceeded suggested that she was well aware she had lost this crucial battle.

By repeating questions, Walden may not have secured direct answers, but he did provoke responses which proved extremely revealing – not just about the circumstances of Mr Lawson's resignation but, more significantly, about the character of our Prime Minister. Indeed the interview was perhaps far more revealing in this respect than it would have been if Mrs Thatcher had given the cool, straight-forward answers we can all now dream up for her as we read the text of the questions.

This interview alone could be taken as proof that politicians have not destroyed the political interview. The evidence of the series as a whole is that Britain's politicians are perfectly prepared to engage in political interviews and to observe their clear-cut rules. But that does not mean that their approach to the whole business has not changed over the years. They now know it is their most powerful tool of political persuasion and they have worked out how to use it to their advantage. As a result, without even needing to cheat, they can walk all over interviewers who are insufficiently informed, astute or prepared, or who lack real confidence in what they are doing.

Many politicians, as most of the interviews in this book show, have decided that their best bet is to answer the question as clearly and as cleverly as they can. But the rules of the game do not require them all to take this approach on every occasion. There are bound to be times when evasion seems to suit a politician's book, and, as Bull and Mayer have shown, the politicians of today come well equipped with an elaborate battery of methods of trying it on. Confronted with these stratagems, it is the interviewer's job to frustrate them, not to cry "Foul!" If he is known to be effective at his job, his interviewee will think twice before choosing to mess with him.

All too often today, the interviewer is not as adept at his own craft as the politician he is interviewing. Interviewers can often be seen asking imprecise questions or several different questions wrapped up as one. When an interviewee takes advantage of the opportunities for evasion this presents, he may well find that his interviewer merely moves on to the next question on his list. An interviewee who suggests he should be asked about something else may find that his questioner switches obediently to the subject he has proposed. Great interviews may not result, but we should blame the broadcasters, not the politicians.

Sometimes interviewers seem handicapped by more than slow-wittedness or lack of preparation. They can look unsure whether they really want to challenge the nation's leaders. After all, who elected the interviewer? There is still a lot of deference in Britain, and every interviewer who gives a politician a rough ride can expect a heavy protest mailbag the next day. Some interviewers may wonder whether their bosses will welcome this. They know there are viewers who do not want to be shown their leaders' weak points; these viewers prefer to believe that those who rule their lives have everything under control. The politicians themselves, however, are under no such illusion, and rarely complain about tough questioning, however much they may complain about much else. You can ask the Prime Minister what she thinks of the back-bench view that she is off her trolley. You can ask the Deputy Prime

Minister what he thinks of the idea that he is a sycophant. They may answer, they may evade, but they do not object to the question. During the making of *The Walden Interview*, politicians gave us little cause for complaint. On the whole, we got out of them what we were looking for.

It is because we considered we had extracted so much of interest that this book has been prepared. A great deal of what our interviews revealed seemed to us likely to be of continuing interest to anyone seeking to understand British politics over the next few years. So we have set out here the interviews we considered to be most important, together with an explanatory commentary. They are not necessarily the best interviews we conducted. Ken Livingstone's analysis of the defects of Labour's economic policy gave us a model political interview, but it was not welcome to the Labour Party itself, and two days later he was thrown off the National Executive into the obscurity which, for the moment at least, disqualifies him from inclusion. David Owen's interview, with its offer of a new Alliance in the middle of the Liberal Democrats' conference, created a great fuss at the time, but where is he now? Politics is a harsh business.

It is also immensely fascinating and entertaining. There were those who expected *The Walden Interview*'s relentlessly serious approach to put viewers off. We believed, however, that the more seriously we went about our business, the more absorbing the results would be. At least some of the viewers seemed to agree with us. Over three million people postponed their Sunday lunch to watch both the Thatcher and the Lawson interviews. The audience appreciation index for the Thatcher interview made it the eleventh most well-liked programme of any kind on any channel in the week in which it was transmitted.

It seems that the political interview is not only alive and well; it can also provide a good watch. I hope you will find it can also provide a good read.

DAVID COX
Executive Producer
The Walden Interview

ALL THE PRIME MINISTER'S MEN

MRS THATCHER'S STYLE OF LEADERSHIP gave rise to a question which came to be heard more and more often during her time at Number Ten. Was she capable of working only with yes men? It began to seem to some that the price of her Premiership was that no other figures of independent mind would be allowed to play a part in the governance of the realm. One by one, the men of moment seemed to be either sacked or frozen out of the Thatcher Cabinet. It was not just Mrs Thatcher's doctrinal enemies who disappeared. Even those most closely identified with her thinking, like John Biffen and Norman Tebbit, seemed vulnerable if they dared to challenge her on almost anything. The Cabinet seemed to some to be becoming little more than a rubber stamp for the will of Downing Street, where the Prime Minister shared decision-making, if she shared it at all, with a shadowy bunch of unelected advisers. Critics played on deep-rooted fears of the witch-queen who wields absolute power from amidst a court of fawning sycophants – fears which could be politely expressed as concern for the health of Cabinet government, a concept elevated for the purpose into one of the central planks of the Constitution.

At first, such attacks did Mrs Thatcher little harm. A witch-queen apparently able to cure the long-standing ills of the British economy could be allowed her eccentricities. By the middle of 1989, however, the Thatcher miracle seemed to be evaporating as inflation and balance of payments deficits re-emerged. It was a time when a more cautious leader might have developed a taste for Cabinet government, if only as a means of spreading the blame. Not Mrs Thatcher. She chose this moment to turn upon her closest, longest-standing and least threatening ally, Sir Geoffrey Howe. Sir Geoffrey had done much to develop the ideology of Thatcherism, and, as Chancellor in 1981, he had braved the fires of recession in its name without so much as flinching. Yet, as Foreign Secretary, he found himself at odds with Mrs Thatcher over Europe. He wanted more integration; she did not. And to his and everyone else's surprise, in the Cabinet reshuffle of July 1989 she stripped him of his post. Sir Geoffrey did not however go as quietly as previous victims. In return for accepting demotion to the post of Leader of the House, he extracted the title of Deputy Prime Minister. He won much sympathy in the Cabinet and the Commons, and people began to wonder if he might use the opportunity presented by his new position to break what they saw as the Prime Minister's dictatorial grip. He certainly seemed to have cause to move against her; but he was also thought the mildest of men. Would he rise to what some considered to be his historic task?

This was the kind of question which *The Walden Interview* existed to address. We invited Sir Geoffrey on; and his decision to accept, as sometimes happens, itself provided part of the answer. Had he intended to lick his wounds and lie low, there would have been no point in going on television and telling this to what would have been a somewhat derisive world. Sir Geoffrey clearly intended to run up some sort of flag; but, being Sir Geoffrey, he could be expected to do so only in the most opaque and roundabout way. What kind of questioning would best establish whether Mrs Thatcher really needed to fear him?

We decided that a direct approach was required. We should ask Sir Geoffrey whether he intended to use his new position to curb the Prime Minister's power. If he said no, we should be left with air-time on our hands and egg on our faces. If he said yes, however, we could not leave it at that. It was perfectly possible to imagine Sir Geoffrey committing himself to a bold campaign and then doing nothing to put it into effect. If his intentions sounded positive, we should therefore ask him if he was going to make his presence felt in particular policy areas and whether he was prepared for the Prime Minister's likely response to efforts by her Deputy to cramp her style.

A Deputy Prime Minister declaring war on the Prime Minister in a television interview is not something which happens every day. Yet that is what Sir Geoffrey's downbeat and careful responses can be seen as amounting to. Asked whether he would fight Prime Ministerial resistance to the will of a Cabinet Committee which he chaired, he could have said he was sure any such differences would be swiftly settled over a quiet chat. By claiming instead a constitutional right to take such arguments to full Cabinet, he appeared to be throwing down if not a gauntlet, at least a woolly mitten. When it came to matters on which he might actually make a stand, however, he showed less readiness to do battle. The picture was borne out by subsequent events: in spite of occasional murmurings, seized upon eagerly by the media, Sir Geoffrey's dagger was to stay sheathed, at least for the time being.

Not so Nigel Lawson's. His abrupt departure on 26 October after six years as Chancellor was accompanied by a direct attack on Mrs Thatcher. In his letter of resignation Mr Lawson made it clear that he thought she had undermined him by allowing her economic adviser, Sir Alan Walters, to criticise his policies. It was the prospect that this would continue, he said, which had prompted his resignation. Though high interest rates had made Mr Lawson unpopular, he was recognised as being a more substantial figure than any of the other Cabinet Ministers who had fallen out with the Prime Minister. Concern about Mrs Thatcher's handling of her colleagues reached crisis proportions.

Over two months earlier Mrs Thatcher had agreed to appear on the edition of *The Walden Interview* to be transmitted on 29 October. Unusually, the interview was to be recorded the day before. When we heard of Mr Lawson's resignation on the Thursday evening, we were preparing an interview which already concentrated on Mrs Thatcher's long-standing differences with her Chancellor. We decided we must still ask her what the Government's real position was on the economic questions in dispute, and in the interview she said where she stood on both of the main points of issue – British entry into the exchange rate mechanism of the European Monetary System and exchange rate policy in the interim. But the political question about the way Mrs Thatcher handled her Ministers was clearly much more important. It looked as though the Prime Minister's survival would be in doubt unless she gave some sign that she intended to mend her ways.

We decided that such a sign would need to include some acknowledgement of a share of the blame for Mr Lawson's departure. In the interview, her repeated refusal to make any such acknowledgement could have left no-one in any doubt that what she termed "strong government" would undoubtedly continue for as long as she stayed at Number Ten. Whatever the wisdom of this line, Mrs Thatcher went on to make new difficulties for herself. Seeking to avoid the allegation that she had preferred a part-time adviser to her Chancellor, she said she did not know whether Mr Lawson would have stayed if she had sacked Sir Alan. In view of the content of Mr Lawson's letter of resignation and the fact that he had attended four meetings with her on the day he wrote it, this appeared to cast doubt on either the honesty or the articulacy of a man not generally thought to lack either quality, whatever others he might be short of. So Mrs Thatcher added doubts about her own truthfulness to those about her handling of a key Minister which she had done nothing to dispel.

Naturally, viewers would want to hear Nigel Lawson's side of this story. But how eager would he be to give it? He might want to clear his name, but the price of trying to do so might be to plunge the Government into an even deeper crisis, and many of his friends and former colleagues could be expected to go to some lengths to dissuade him. Mr Lawson had however agreed to come on the following week's programme before the Thatcher interview took place, and during that interview Walden had announced that he would be asking Mr Lawson for his account of events. Pulling out of an interview is a different matter from declining to appear in one: had Mr Lawson withdrawn, this might have been interpreted as implying that he accepted Mrs Thatcher's account of what had transpired.

Whether or not Mr Lawson relished the position in which he found himself on 5 November, he had clearly decided that if he was going to have to give his version he should do the job properly. We had prepared for a whole variety of different ways in which Mr Lawson might try to duck the questions. In the event, the only problem was that his answers were so lucid and to the point that Walden got through the questions much faster than we expected. There was no room for ambiguity: Mr Lawson said he resigned because Mrs Thatcher had refused his demand that Sir Alan Waters should go by the end of the year. Asked how she could have been in doubt about his position, he could only suggest that she must have thought he had been bluffing. It was an explanation which acquitted Mrs Thatcher of the charge of lying, but suggested that her problems of man management were not only all too real but were now also compounded by self-delusion.

3RD SEPTEMBER, 1989

BRIAN WALDEN INTERVIEWS SIR GEOFFREY HOWE

BRIAN WALDEN:
Just six weeks ago, Sir Geoffrey Howe became Britain's Deputy Prime Minister. Mrs Thatcher didn't give him the job willingly, he had to demand it as his price for going along with her Cabinet reshuffle. The whole extraordinary episode has aroused keen interest in the way in which Sir Geoffrey intends to use his new position. Does he want to become a counter-weight to Mrs Thatcher in the government, or will he allow himself to be used simply as a mere functionary? Sir Geoffrey Howe is here today to tell me.

Sir Geoffrey, there has been an immense amount of interest in your job and how you intend to do it, a lot of it interested and expectant, some of it dismissive. Let me ask you directly, how do you see your role as Deputy Prime Minister?

SIR GEOFFREY HOWE:
I think as I've always seen it, really: a member of a strong long-distance-running Conservative team, designed to sustain the momentum of the revolution that we set in hand, now many years ago. I've always tried to put my whole weight behind that in the way in which I judge most effective, in whatever position I'm in.

BRIAN WALDEN:
And as a member of a team?

SIR GEOFFREY HOWE:
Certainly. I think that the success we've achieved as a government has depended upon teamwork, and on partnership; on the presentation of policies by more than one person, by the analysis by the government as a whole. It's not possible to do it in any other way.

BRIAN WALDEN:
All right, now let me put this to you . . . you see, there are many things that Deputy Prime Ministers have to do, they're part of the job specification – they have to be ready to be consulted, give advice when it's solicited, etcetera, etcetera. And you'll do all of that, I'm sure. But looking at the history of Deputy Prime Ministers, there are two ways of playing it. One is in fact to make it quite clear that you have no views that you wish to express in public, to keep your head well down, to act as a sort of functionary, and keep the wheels greased. The other is to take a much more independent role, to let it be known that in extremis there is a Deputy Prime Minister there who, if he thinks the interests of the party or indeed the country, demand it, is prepared to fight, is prepared to say "No, we must do this". Now, which way are you going to play it, Sir Geoffrey?

SIR GEOFFREY HOWE:
Well, I've never been a politician who has actually hidden his intellectual light under a bushel, although some people think so. If you look at the pattern of my behaviour during our ten years in government and many years before that, I have made a practice – I suppose because I can hardly give it up – of analysing, presenting, making speeches, writing pamphlets and so on. I have done that during my time at the Foreign Office and at the Treasury, every few months, because I think it's very important that people should see that there is within the government a group of people thinking ahead, looking ahead. I shall go on doing that, and I think that it's quite clear from my track record that I will not be concerned to submerge that, but I shall be presenting that as part of the thinking process, which is very important.

BRIAN WALDEN:
So you are not going to play a submerged role, you are going to play an independent active role.

SIR GEOFFREY HOWE:
An independent and active role as part of a team. One needs both. But the system can't work unless you are all working for a common objective. That has been the great joy of working for the last fifteen years, as we have done in opposition and in office – that we have tackled objectives and purposes that other people find impossible. Objectives that you and I have tackled in our different ways in the past. And we've been able to succeed in overcoming many of them.

BRIAN WALDEN:
But, and I'm not stressing it unnecessarily, but you know the essence of some of the problems here. Of course, there has to be a measure of agreement. No side can go on a pitch unless it is prepared to have some

measure of agreement, but I notice that the emphasis in your mind is towards activity and independence, isn't it?

SIR GEOFFREY HOWE:
It's towards activity, and as much independence as I think makes sense. Again, if one spends one's life attracting attention as a kind of diverse fragmentary influence in the party, one is not achieving one's purpose. So within the party, within government, within parliament, within the party and the country, within the nation as a whole, one goes on arguing for the things we are trying to achieve, and they are common objectives carrying through and sustaining the revolution that we have carried through in the last ten years.

BRIAN WALDEN:
All right, now let me just a little . . . because there is a lot to discuss obviously, there are serious policy issues later on . . . but let me test that – what you have just said about activity – against likely scenarios. For instance you are going to chair, a number of Cabinet committees – and they are important ones too – supposing, one of those Cabinet committees comes up with a proposition that the Prime Minister doesn't like and she announces she is thinking of overruling it. Now will you accept that or will you fight?

SIR GEOFFREY HOWE:
The position is provided for by the constitution, that Cabinet committees look at matters within their range of responsibility. They then come with agreed or disagreed recommendations for further consideration by the Cabinet and, as we have done in the past, we shall have discussions of them there. It is very important that there should be that discussion because I think that . . .

BRIAN WALDEN:
In the Cabinet?

SIR GEOFFREY HOWE:
Everywhere. You see, if you are right about what you are trying to do, then you need to extend the range of those who agree with you. You need to win arguments, win friends for the policy. Now that may mean adjusting the policy. It may mean getting it acceptable as well as workable, but that's part of the discussion that takes place within government.

BRIAN WALDEN:
Let me be clear that I haven't misunderstood you, Sir Geoffrey. You are saying: you are chairing this Cabinet committee, that that committee arrives at a decision, the Prime Minister says: "I am very sorry Geoffrey, I don't like it. I'm not going to have that." You will then go to the Cabinet and argue for the Cabinet committee's point of view.

SIR GEOFFREY HOWE:
Yes. It doesn't happen like that, you see. The Cabinet committee . . .

BRIAN WALDEN:
I know, but that's why I want you to tell me how it's going to happen.

SIR GEOFFREY HOWE:
The Cabinet committee is a group of Cabinet colleagues. They don't find themselves addressing a problem unless it's been considered quite a long way down the system, through the system, before you get to that point, and you will have been discussing it in embryo, in conception, with the Prime Minister and his (sic) colleagues all the way through. So you decide first of all: is this a topic we have to tackle? Are we going to try and tackle it this term, next term or whatever? Then you get to the difficult bits, about actually working out how you get round that corner, how you make it acceptable. But it isn't something that suddenly arrives from the bosom of a Cabinet committee on the table of the et, unheralded and unexpected. It's a symbiotic process and it has to stay like that.

BRIAN WALDEN:
Accepting that it . . . what a lovely word . . . accepting that it is a symbiotic process, it isn't quite as simple as you're putting it, Geoffrey. Disagreements can arise, they can arise about timing and all the rest of it . . . what I want to get out of you is, if the Prime Minister says, "I am very sorry, Sir Geoffrey, I'm not having that", are you going to say, "All right Prime Minister, you're the boss, that's it" or are you going to say, "No, I'm sorry Prime Minister, I think we ought to thrash this out in Cabinet"?

SIR GEOFFREY HOWE:
Well that's what one must say, and what one has said . . .

BRIAN WALDEN:
The second – that one must thrash this out in Cabinet?

SIR GEOFFREY HOWE:
Because, because colleagues are accustomed to doing that. Cabinet exists for that purpose, and issues of importance and difficulty are taken there, sometimes without a great expectation of a long debate because the debate's already gone a long way along the road, but if there's an anxiety to be cleared, then it has to be cleared in Cabinet, and it is.

BRIAN WALDEN:
And you would think it entirely constitutional, and in no way unscrupulous and nothing to worry about, to rally Cabinet colleagues if necessary against the Prime Minister's veto on what you'd done?

SIR GEOFFREY HOWE:
That's a dramatic way of putting it, and again it's not the way in which it happens.

BRIAN WALDEN:
All right.

SIR GEOFFREY HOWE:
It's not a question of rallying Cabinet colleagues against the Prime Minister's veto, it's having a discussion with the whole Cabinet on the basis of what is the right answer, what is the right approach, and Cabinet comes to a conclusion on it in that setting, but it's not a question of rallying them in a dissident style.

BRIAN WALDEN:
All right. I admit, yes, I put it to you in perhaps its most difficult form, but let me be quite clear about what I am putting to you, and let me be quite clear about your answer. Though done courteously, though it is understood it was going to happen, you'll be arguing for one point of view, and the Prime Minister will be arguing for a different one in some cases, and you're not worried about that. You think it's perfectly constitutional, and perfectly all right.

SIR GEOFFREY HOWE:
But this is a picture that over-dramatises life in Cabinet, because it suggests that this is a pattern of regular occurrence.

BRIAN WALDEN:
But could it ever happen?

SIR GEOFFREY HOWE:
It could happen.

BRIAN WALDEN:
It could happen.

SIR GEOFFREY HOWE:
It has happened. It has happened under this government and under other governments, because that's the sensible way of discussing an issue.

BRIAN WALDEN:
This isn't going to keep you awake at nights, is it? If these occasional disagreements have to happen, and you occasionally have to say, "Well, I'm sorry Prime Minister, no, I want this discussed in the Cabinet."?

SIR GEOFFREY HOWE:
No, and if you think about other difficult decisions that we've taken together, the whole range of fiscal policies and budgetary policies we carried through during the first parliament, the abolition of exchange control, the installation of the medium term financial strategy, all those things required a great deal of discussion not just in Cabinet but in discussion between the Chancellor of the Exchequer and the Prime Minister. And we came or sought to come to common conclusions about them. That's what life is about. It's very important that it should be on that broad basis, because unless you have got the bugs out of an argument first in private, if there's a difference, you aren't going to be able to sustain the case in public thereafter.

BRIAN WALDEN:
I understand that. You said a little bit earlier, Sir Geoffrey, that you'd played a very large part in all sorts of things for a very long time, and that's absolutely true, of course. Some people say that you are the inventor of much that the Government has presently done. You were Chancellor for four years, Foreign Secretary for six, and all that. Let me put something to you which could sound offensive, if it weren't for the fact that you know I'm not trying to be offensive. An idea has got around that you're a kind of . . . of sycophant – it's partly because of your quiet personality, and all that, and that the Prime Minister is going to just shove you all over the place. She'll just dish out her orders and Geoffrey will run through the door and carry them out. Now, what you've said earlier makes it quite clear that you don't see it like that at all, do you?

SIR GEOFFREY HOWE:
It never has been like that, you see. You were kind enough to apologise for the offensiveness . . . it's part of the common stock in trade of many commentators to say: "Oh, Geoffrey will always go along with what the Prime Minister wants, that's the way it's always been" . . . It never has been like that because . . .

BRIAN WALDEN:
And is it going to be in future?

SIR GEOFFREY HOWE:
Well, because we have been in the business of taking difficult decisions together, starting if I may say so, from a position in which we, and two or three others, were in a minority in intellectual analysis in the Conservative Party, and we had to secure the acceptance of the kind of radical approach that we've followed in the last ten years. So, a great deal of it has taken place in partnership.

BRIAN WALDEN:
Sure.

SIR GEOFFREY HOWE:
But in the course of that partnership of course there have been disagreements. And . . .

BRIAN WALDEN:
And will there be again?

SIR GEOFFREY HOWE:
I have no doubt there will be some . . . there always are in any relationship.

BRIAN WALDEN:
And this is not keeping you awake at nights? You're not terrified of Mrs Thatcher, trembling to go in and tell her that you don't agree with her?

SIR GEOFFREY HOWE:
No, we've been in business together for a long time, and as I say we're amongst the founder members of what we've been doing and have achieved a great deal together . . . not just two of us, for heaven's sake . . .

BRIAN WALDEN:
Of course not.

SIR GEOFFREY HOWE:
. . . in partnership with a whole range of colleagues who've been with us.

BRIAN WALDEN:
I understand that. But you're a Deputy Prime Minister now and this is an intimate and close relationship. I have to put this to you. There are public images of you which you're making quite clear you don't think by any means are exact. There are also public images of the Prime Minister – one of them is that she doesn't want to listen to anybody, and least of all does she want to listen to the Deputy Prime Minister, so that when you go in and tell her something, what she will do in fact is bang the table and order you out. What about that?

SIR GEOFFREY HOWE:
Yes, that again is another of these satirical pictures that gets around. The fact is that the Prime Minister is a person of very strong views, very clear thinking, very strong sense of purpose and she has a conviction that a lot of the things she believes in are right. Well, so do we all. And in those circumstances, she, as you, as I, respect those people who are prepared to say: "But, look, it isn't like that." Now there are different ways of

doing it, there are different ways of having a discussion of that kind, which depends upon the chemistry of the group, the people you are talking about. But we have never found it impossible at any stage, to discuss matters and reach conclusions about them that are compatible with a continuing working relationship.

BRIAN WALDEN:
Even where there have been disagreements and arguments?

SIR GEOFFREY HOWE:
No, of course there have been arguments.

BRIAN WALDEN:
You've never raised your voice to her?

SIR GEOFFREY HOWE:
Not much more often than I have to other people, which is not very often.

BRIAN WALDEN:
But you have.

SIR GEOFFREY HOWE:
I don't think my voice is to be judged by the number of decibels it emits.

BRIAN WALDEN:
True.

SIR GEOFFREY HOWE:
I believe that . . .

BRIAN WALDEN:
But you have made quite clear your disagreement with what she thinks on a particular thing.

SIR GEOFFREY HOWE:
Of course, because . . .

BRIAN WALDEN:
And you are going to again if you have to?

SIR GEOFFREY HOWE:
For . . . a whole range of decisions that have been taken by us over the years together have required that kind of analysis, in which we have had to come to a common conclusion. And so, so it will be.

BRIAN WALDEN:
I've got one problem about this, Sir Geoffrey, in that I recall something which she said before she ever came to power, and it's stuck, I'm afraid, it's stuck. It gets quoted again and again and again – that she can't afford any time for disagreements in her Cabinet. They've got to get on with it. There she is, she's got her policies, she'll tell them what they are, it's all got to be brisk and quick, no time for any arguments. Now, what about this? If she's got no time for any arguments, how do you ever get to the point where you can have one with her?

SIR GEOFFREY HOWE:
That, I think was a figure of speech.

BRIAN WALDEN:
But she said it though, didn't she?

SIR GEOFFREY HOWE:
Of course she said it . . . we've all said a lot of things like that from time to time . . .

BRIAN WALDEN:
She was wrong to say it, wasn't she?

SIR GEOFFREY HOWE:
Well, because that is not life as it has been lived under ten years of Margaret Thatcher's premiership.

BRIAN WALDEN:
And it isn't life as it's going to be lived?

SIR GEOFFREY HOWE:
No, it's not life as it can be lived. Of course, she makes plain when she has a strong view about something, we all know that very clearly, but the purpose of working together in Cabinet is to be able to discuss things even so and reach conclusions which you can carry forward together. You aren't going to carry forward the policies which have been as radical and as revolutionary as we have done over the last ten years without carrying people with you. Government, democratic government, is government by explanation and you have to do that by explaining to the people at large what you're doing. Now, if you're going to do that at all then of course you have to discuss and explain within government, and that's recognised by Margaret Thatcher, one of the greatest democratic leaders in history. People don't begin to challenge her capacity for identifying what people are concerned about and trying to distill that into practical policies.

BRIAN WALDEN:
But they do – they do challenge whether she's prepared to listen to anyone in the world. There's a general . . . there's a *Spitting Image* view around that she isn't, that you're all eunuchs and you're told what to do by her and if anybody dissents that's it, they're out.

SIR GEOFFREY HOWE:
Yes, well, that's . . . leave that to *Spitting Image,* because life is not like that. On the other hand you'll find that any strong, effective political leader has to maintain strength and sense of purpose, and from time to time that is bound to give the impression of less than total tolerance for every point of view under the sun. But that's life again.

BRIAN WALDEN:
All right. Earlier on I put to you a scenario that you said was rather extreme and that the real world didn't work like that, and I accepted it because I put it to you for a purpose. Let me put another thing to you for a purpose which is also extreme. This is a very extreme case indeed, but if the disagreement was so fundamental that you felt a vital point of principle was involved which affected the issues of the Conservative Party, which affected how it might do in elections, and its future and all the rest of it, you're still prepared to resign, aren't you Sir Geoffrey?

SIR GEOFFREY HOWE:
Everyone in politics at every level retains that option, but it is close to being the politician's nuclear weapon. It's not something one goes around thinking about any more than one finds onself taking decisions day after day that keep you awake at night. One has to sustain a case and recognise that the strength of one's position depends upon the strength of the team you're being able to persuade.

BRIAN WALDEN:
Well, you know why I asked you – and I'll make this because I want to move on to something else, we want to come to some of the practical problems you'll have to face – but I asked you for a fairly simple reason. I'll put it to you quite bluntly. You are not the kind of man who can just be shoved from pillar to post and just do as he's told and never say: "Look, no, sorry I've had enough of that, if I can't get my way on this I shall resign." In extremis you would say that, wouldn't you?

SIR GEOFFREY HOWE:
I must say that because any politician who has any credibility at all must say that and believe it, but it's not my purpose nor my objective, nor near the front of my mind, nor has it even been. I'm in politics for the sake of carrying through, over a wider and wider field, the enormously successful polices we've followed. When we started on them . . . thinking

about them fifteen years back, Britain was at the bottom of the pit and going down, and nobody had any hope for us whatsoever. We have put them in place and carried them through and in all my work as Foreign Secretary I saw country after country, from the Soviet Union to the People's Republic of China, reaching out to follow our example. And what we're trying now is to spread the successes we've achieved in economic terms, to make them more effective – for heaven's sake, there's still a huge economic agenda to overcome – and to spread them wider into the social field as well.

BRIAN WALDEN:
All right, now let's get on to agendas. I think what you've said so far will surprise a great many people. You may think it ought not to but it will. What we see is a robust Deputy Prime Minister who has an agenda, who has things he wants to do and is prepared to fight for them – let me now bring you to the practicalities of that. Let us test this robust Deputy Premier against these problems, starting by my telling you – which will come to you as no great surprise, Geoffrey – that things could be better for the Conservative Party. You had a bad Euro-election, Labour's ahead on the polls, a lot of people think Labour looks more electable than it used to, some of your back benchers have got a bit of the jitters . . . do you accept that the Government has got real problems that it's got to confront?

SIR GEOFFREY HOWE:
The Government, after having been in office for as long as we have, has got the crucially important problem of sustaining our momentum, securing our re-election. Now, granted that we've been doing this for so long, I think the remarkable thing is that the Labour Party, which has had more than a decade in which to reconstruct itself, can command such a modest lead in the opinion polls.

BRIAN WALDEN:
Enough to win, though?

SIR GEOFFREY HOWE:
Well, enough to win but, for heavens sake, the BBC average of polls on Friday night/Saturday morning was talking about a 3% average. Now I'm not complacent at all . . . but that's . . .

BRIAN WALDEN:
Ah, I'm glad to hear that. I was just going to ask you that very question.

SIR GEOFFREY HOWE:
No, but that's hardly the commanding lead you'd expect a credible opposition to have built up by this time.

BRIAN WALDEN:
Possibly, but you've got problems yourself as a government, haven't you? Come on, it's not all rosy is it?

SIR GEOFFREY HOWE:
Of course not, but they're problems . . . let me take them in two halves. There are problems that we as Britain still face despite the massive success of the last ten years . . . if one takes our economic performance, the Labour government that you supported way back in the 60s would have given its eye teeth to have achieved eight years' growth of the kind that we've had over the last eight years, dramatic success in expanding and restoring our industrial strength . . .

BRIAN WALDEN:
Sure, but Geoffrey, you're going to do some wonderful party political broadcasts on exactly that theme and no doubt there'll be much truth in them . . . I'm much more interested not in the things that have gone right but in the things that have gone wrong.

SIR GEOFFREY HOWE:
But, forgive me, I want to just make the point I was making, because I was going to go on to say, not that this has gone wrong, but we still have a very long way to go. If you take the strength and health of our industrial sector, we have saved from perdition industries that would have . . . would have destroyed themselves like the motorcycle industry. The automobile industry is a very good example. But for heaven's sake, we still aren't commanding 50% of our own automobile market. We are producing a great many more motor cars now than at the end of the Labour government . . .

BRIAN WALDEN:
Well, alright, I'm . . .

SIR GEOFFREY HOWE:
But, the point I'm making is this . . .

BRIAN WALDEN:
I do understand the point you're making . . .

SIR GEOFFREY HOWE:
. . . that there's a huge sustained pressure to be kept up.

BRIAN WALDEN:
I'm a little bit more . . . I'm a little bit worried about the fact that we're not commanding 50% of our own automobile market, but I tell you something that's worrying Tory backbenchers a lot more than that, and

that's a number of things: poll tax, National Health Service, we'll come to them – let me ask you first the whole way the government takes its decisions. I suppose the commonest complaint I hear from Tory back-benchers is that there isn't enough team work, it's all too ad hoc. It isn't the Cabinet that you were talking about earlier – the Cabinet discussing, the Cabinet deciding – there's a widespread feeling on your own back benches that the Cabinet doesn't decide, that even Cabinet committees don't always decide, that it's all done ad hoc. Now do you think that that's a worry that you ought to try to at least ease?

SIR GEOFFREY HOWE:
I think it's a worry that you can identify. I think it's largely misplaced. If you take for example the community charge, one of the stock areas of anxiety, nobody is now arguing that reform along those lines was not necessary. The decision to achieve that reform was ground through . . .

BRIAN WALDEN:
You mean in the Conservative Party they're not?

SIR GEOFFREY HOWE:
Yes.

BRIAN WALDEN:
All right. Your political opponents don't think it was necessary?

SIR GEOFFREY HOWE:
No, but . . . but . . . but beyond that, our political opponents are very short in alternatives. Nobody is defending the system that exists, everyone acknowledges that change had to be undertaken and the central decisions about that have been talked about and thought about and analysed within government and within the Party for a very long time . . .

BRIAN WALDEN:
Sure.

SIR GEOFFREY HOWE:
We still haven't finished that . . .

BRIAN WALDEN:
Ah well, hang on you see, Nick . . . you say poll tax as if this was somehow a good idea . . . Nick Budgen, one of your own MPs says it's a dagger pointed at the political heart of the Conservative Party. They're very unhappy about it. Have you got any suggestions that might ease their mind about the poll tax, Sir Geoffrey?

SIR GEOFFREY HOWE:
Well, Nick is a master of dramatic advocacy and one has to take seriously his anxiety obviously and we all do . . .

BRIAN WALDEN:
Lot to be said for dramatic advocacy, you know.

SIR GEOFFREY HOWE:
Yes well, I'm making no complaint about it, but the fact is that nobody challenges the importance of making a change . . . we have to get away from a system of . . .

BRIAN WALDEN:
All right, but can you ease their mind a bit? They're very worried about it . . .

SIR GEOFFREY HOWE:
But look, let me finish making my point.

BRIAN WALDEN:
Sure.

SIR GEOFFREY HOWE:
They now recognise we have moved to a system that is fairer, more comprehensive, more likely to make the elected local authorities accountable to their electors than that which has gone before. They're concerned as to whether the margins of it are right. They're concerned as anyone must be with any major tax reform of the fact that there are going to be losers. Well there's no escape from that.

BRIAN WALDEN:
Sure.

SIR GEOFFREY HOWE:
You can't have a tax reform without having some shift in the burden, and if you're making it fairer then there have to be changes. I think they're concerned that at each stage of its implementation we should be alert to the appearance of removable errors, and the Prime Minister herself has said that the new Environment Secretary, Chris Patten, will be looking at it again.

BRIAN WALDEN:
Have *you* been looking at it again, privately? I mean, I'm asking you quite bluntly, have you got . . . all right it isn't government policy yet, the Cabinet haven't discussed it . . . but have you got a suggestion as to how the situation might be eased?

SIR GEOFFREY HOWE:
I have been looking at it again more closely now that I'm back on the home front, so to speak . . .

BRIAN WALDEN:
Sure.

SIR GEOFFREY HOWE:
. . . than when . . . than I was able to do when I was in the Foreign Office, and my conclusion is that the essential features of it are inescapably right if you are to achieve the two objectives . . .

BRIAN WALDEN:
Or anyway inescapable . . .

SIR GEOFFREY HOWE:
No, inescapably right. If you are to make it fairer, if you are to make it a more accountable system, then something along these lines that enlarge the number of people who pay taxes, as compared to those who vote in local elections, had to be undertaken. And we looked at the others many times in the decade or more that's gone before, and it's very difficult to think of any one that would be better than this. But people are now looking, quite understandably, whether in county halls or in constituencies or in MPs' mail bags, at just how it's going to work out for their folk, for folk of this kind or that kind. Now, many of the details that will enable us to answer that question are not yet in place. It's absolutely right there should be . . .

BRIAN WALDEN:
Let me put some suggestions . . . you see, okay, the poll tax, you say is a fine thing. You say it was inevitable and I'm bound to add that there'd have had to be a re-rating anyway . . .

SIR GEOFFREY HOWE:
Well, that's the point.

BRIAN WALDEN:
So, yes, exactly . . .

SIR GEOFFREY HOWE:
The grass is always greener on the other side of the valley.

BRIAN WALDEN:
Yes . . . yes . . . now let's come back. You're the Leader of the House and the Deputy Prime Minister . . . a roaring, I am told an unprecedented ovation, never anything like it in my time, from your own backbenchers

. . . they're looking to you. Let me put some ideas for you, which you can't say, "Yes that's what the Cabinet will do", but you can say, "I, Sir Geoffrey, think there might be something in that". One is about this safety net, the transitional arrangement whereby for four years the low spending Tory councils have got to shove money over to the high spending Labour councils. Sir Geoffrey, couldn't the Exchequer assume that burden so that the Tory councils didn't have to? Is that something you're thinking about?

SIR GEOFFREY HOWE:
Two things to say first of all about that. This isn't a novelty, it's what has always happened under the system we're replacing, and in the process of . . .

BRIAN WALDEN:
But that's why you're supposed to be replacing it, so that it doesn't happen.

SIR GEOFFREY HOWE:
Yes, but again Brian, let me finish the point.

BRIAN WALDEN:
Sure.

SIR GEOFFREY HOWE:
That is part of the system that's always been there. In course of the change as so far proposed, the Exchequer is already taking on board part of the continuing cost of that. The matter . . .

BRIAN WALDEN:
Why not take the lot?

SIR GEOFFREY HOWE:
Well, why not take the lot, now that's redolent of the view that the Exchequer, by throwing another billion at everything, can always relieve us of all our troubles and that's simply not right.

BRIAN WALDEN:
No, but it might on this one, mightn't it . . . get you right off the hook of the thing being a muddle, enormously pleases the Tory backbenchers and gets them to accept all the stuff that you were telling me earlier about what a wonderful thing the poll tax is.

SIR GEOFFREY HOWE:
Yes, but Brian . . .

BRIAN WALDEN:
It's worth a billion, isn't it?

SIR GEOFFREY HOWE:
No, forgive me Brian, that is so seductive but so grossly oversimplified. The position is this – Chris Patten took over this dossier from Nick Ridley at the end of July . . . er . . . clearly the details of many parts of it are still to be put in place, and the safety net and the way that works is one of the things, along with many others, that he is examining and looking at . . .

BRIAN WALDEN:
Ah, and if he . . . if he came to you . . . you say what I say is grossly exaggerated, well, we shall see, we shall see . . . supposing Chris Patten, one of your colleagues, came to you and said: "Well, Geoffrey, I've come to the view that we have got to fund all of this out of the Exchequer, it makes more sense, it's more logical, it gives the poll tax more meaning and it will cheer up our back-benchers." Would you stand in his way and say, "Oh no, no, no, I can't possibly have that" or would you be inclined to listen to him and push for it?

SIR GEOFFREY HOWE:
No, I can never imagine myself answering a question like that with such simplicity. The fact is that all my commitment over the last decade has been to secure sustainable, steady economic progress. Part of that has been to secure a steady reduction in the percentage of wealth going to the state. Now, if I begin responding to every bid put to me in that beguiling simple form by saying, "Yes give him the money, Barney," we destroy the programme, we destroy my credibility, we destroy everything else. All I can say is that along with many other attractively competing suggestions, if such a proposal was made it would have to be looked at, not just by me but by all of us.

BRIAN WALDEN:
All right, let me give you another suggestion. What you could do is reduce the actual amount of poll tax that people have to pay by switching some of the charge from local to national taxation. An oft quoted example, wildly popular on your back-benches by the way, the chaps who you're supposed to be soothing, is to switch the whole burden of education from local charge to national charge. Now how do you feel about that one?

SIR GEOFFREY HOWE:
Well, again it fails to take account of the fact that a very very large proportion, I think it's about three quarters of the total expenditure of local government, is going to be met from sources other than the poll tax.

It's going to be met from the business rate and from the grant that is received from the Exchequer. So that if you take account of the fact that three quarters of everything being spent by local government is already funded from elsewhere, and I think I'm right in saying that only two thirds of it is related to education, we've gone virtually down that road by a different means anyway. What we have left is about a quarter of the total cost to local government, to be met from the community charge, being paid by a much much larger range of electors than previously, so that all of them will be taking some part in achieving more responsibility at local government. Now I don't think one can make any fundamental shift in that. What we're talking about is discussion of seeing this legitimate and important change through, after we've looked at the details. And of course everyone will be doing that.

BRIAN WALDEN:
All right, there might, there might . . . not very forthcoming on that, but there might be some changes when you've looked at the details. Let me try about health. The health service reforms, so called, are wildly unpopular and doing the government enormous damage. Now is there anything that you could suggest that would improve the situation there?

SIR GEOFFREY HOWE:
I think . . . a closer understanding of the proposals already put forward, after further debate. I'm very struck . . . Let me tell you . . .

BRIAN WALDEN:
Sir Geoffrey, the more you talk about them the more votes you lose. The clearer your intention becomes the more the public hates it.

SIR GEOFFREY HOWE:
No, that . . .

BRIAN WALDEN:
That's what the polls seem to say . . .

SIR GEOFFREY HOWE:
No, with . . . if that were remotely true then we shouldn't be in the position we are now with a modest lead on the Labour Party. That's the reality. If the things were anything like the caricature you've presented that would simply not be the case. Now let me tell you this about the Health Service changes. One of my first jobs way back in the 60s in Parliament, which was fulfilling a long term interest, was to be a shadow front bench spokesman on health and social security matters. I became in that job again ten years later in '75 and I've always been intensely interested in the process of freeing up the rigidity of the structure of the National Health Service, giving those who practice in it a greater sense

of control over their own resources and how it's run. I've canvassed and looked at all sorts of proposals on all sorts of committees over all that time. I now come back to look with some care at what is proposed in the White Paper and I'm very impressed with what is being put forward. It's not been put forward by extraordinary people from outer space – Ken Clark was one of my first PPSs, David Mellor was a close colleague in the Foreign Office, they have all taken part in the analysis of it. What is there, is in principle welcomed by a very wide range of people.

BRIAN WALDEN:
Who for instance? The nurses hate it, the doctors hate it, the public hates it, the BMA's running an enormous campaign against it, your own backbenchers are frightened to death with how many votes it's losing, who likes it?

SIR GEOFFREY HOWE:
Quite frankly the BMA, the BMA campaign is the most striking feature. Almost every newspaper in the country this week has said in the plainest terms that the BMA campaign has gone over the top in terms of intemperance and addressing itself to the real issues. If you look in today's papers you'll find a very very classic illustration of it, because the BMA – it's an article in the *Sunday Express* – says that what the Government has done has been to add to a legitimate purpose of trying to reform the structure of it, two things that are wholly intolerable, wholly bad ideas. One is the self-governing hospital, the other is the practice budget, and it is intolerable that these things should be imposed, says the BMA, in this article. Why not – let me make the point – why not, they say, let us have these tried out as pilots to see if they work. On the very same page an article by Ken Clark is saying that no hospital and no doctor, no practitioner will be required to take part in those things, only those who volunteer can take part in those deliberately presented experimental things. Now this is why the advocacy, it seems to me, of those who oppose change has succeeded in presenting a totally misleading position.

BRIAN WALDEN:
All right. Sir Geoffrey, we are coming towards the end of this part. I want to come back and ask you some different things, but I don't think it's an unfair summary to say that you *are* going to be an active Deputy Prime Minister, and you *do* show a robust view of all this, but on specifics you're very much keeping your own counsel at the moment. In the second part, I'd like to talk to you about some of the consequences of that.

. . . .

BRIAN WALDEN:
Sir Geoffrey, you're holding your policy cards very close to your chest, as indeed one would expect. We've both been around quite some time, and it would be very odd indeed if the Deputy Prime Minister announced a completely new agenda without having discussed it with the Cabinet and all that. Though it's pretty obvious the way your mind is moving, and it's pretty obvious that you do intend to take a rather *robust* role and also a very active role in the sense that you're going to talk about this, and you're going to listen to Chris Patten on that, and you've got your Cabinet committees and sub-committees to chair – sixteen in all, I think. Let me put this to you, because it will be said, and it might as well be said straight out and laid on the table: if you really are going to do the job well, the job of Deputy Prime Minister well, the Prime Minister herself ain't going to like that one bit, is she?

SIR GEOFFREY HOWE:
I don't think that's a fair analysis at all, if I may say so.

BRIAN WALDEN:
But it will be said, won't it?

SIR GEOFFREY HOWE:
It'll be said . . .

BRIAN WALDEN:
Well what's your answer?

SIR GEOFFREY HOWE:
All sorts of things will be said, and you've omitted a most important feature of the role of Deputy Prime Minister, and that is the presentation of the policies to which we're already committed. You suggest that I'm holding policy options close to my chest . . . what I find is interesting and impressive is that the reforms that we're carrying through in the crucial areas of education and health, for example, are reforms of the kind for which I have pressed and campaigned for decades . . .

BRIAN WALDEN:
Some of them you thought up first, didn't you?

SIR GEOFFREY HOWE:
Well, to some extent, yes, but then a lot of us have been in that business . . .

BRIAN WALDEN:
A Thatcherite before Thatcher?

SIR GEOFFREY HOWE:
I'm not prepared to accept or deny that, it's a . . .

BRIAN WALDEN:
In other words you do accept it.

SIR GEOFFREY HOWE:
It's a compliment if you put it like that . . . and the fact is that if you take schools, for example, I have long thought that it was a great tragedy . . .

BRIAN WALDEN:
But Geoffrey, I don't want to take schools. I want you to tell me why the Prime Minister won't be very angry indeed if you do your job well.

SIR GEOFFREY HOWE:
Because she, I think, will recognise – as I hope the Party will recognise – that what I'm doing is to try and sustain the revolution to which we've been committed for a long time: the revolution of, of realism. Remember I . . . I made a crack in my Party Conference speech last year, that all the -isms where -wasms apart from Thatcherism. Now, I'm still in that business. It's most important that what we have achieved should be sustained. And we're pressing now into areas like the Health Service, so that the small group of people, whether in health or education, who had the freedom of operating in the private sector . . . they used to be regarded as a kind of disreputable Victorian rump . . .

BRIAN WALDEN:
Sure.

SIR GEOFFREY HOWE:
I always thought it was very important that the way in which *they* had access to more choice, and rising standards of care and efficiency, should be more widely extended, should be a bridgehead. Well now, what Kenneth Clark is proposing for the Health Service is in a way providing, within the framework of a publicly funded Health Service, mechanisms for doing that. Doctors and nurses will be able – and some of them are reaching out for the opportunity – to run the show as they want it, more than they've been able to in the past.

BRIAN WALDEN:
Yes, I know, Geoffrey, it's all very splendid, but read me this riddle. You see, this is what interests me, this is what it's all about. Those Tory back-benchers didn't cheer you by accident, they cheered you because they want your influence exerted. Now I want to know, if you say exerting that influence is not going to cause the Prime Minister to be very angry, why she didn't give you the job in the first place, which she didn't. You

had to fight for it. They say you had to make call after call to get all the appurtenances of it, and the Whitehall committees, and all the rest of it. Then Bernard Ingham is put up to rubbish it, and say you may have got it, but it isn't much of a job anyway. What evidence have the public got, or the Conservative Party got, that the . . . that Mrs Thatcher wants you to conduct this job vigorously and actively, and get what you want?

SIR GEOFFREY HOWE:
Well let me dismiss as parody built upon parody the picture you presented earlier on. The fact is that the changes in government made in July resulted in my holding my present position at the request of the Prime Minister . . .

BRIAN WALDEN:
At your insistence . . . you had to ask for it, didn't you?

SIR GEOFFREY HOWE:
Again, it's a matter that has emerged from the changes that took place. I am determined, the Prime Minister is determined that we should make the most of the addition that adds to our strength and effectiveness . . .

BRIAN WALDEN:
But she didn't want it in the first place, did she, Geoffrey? She didn't offer you the job?

SIR GEOFFREY HOWE:
I . . . I'm not prepared to . . .

BRIAN WALDEN:
You grabbed it . . .

SIR GEOFFREY HOWE:
I'm not prepared to discuss that, Brian, because that again is a parody. The fact is . . .

BRIAN WALDEN:
It isn't a parody, you grabbed it. She didn't say "Be Deputy Prime Minister, Geoffrey." You said "I want to be Deputy Prime Minister", didn't you?

SIR GEOFFREY HOWE:
The fact is that I have come back from six years' involvement in foreign affairs to a position, not an unimportant one, domestic affairs, working alongside the Prime Minister, seeking to present and promote our policies as a whole. I like that opportunity, the Conservative Party in Parliament apparently welcomes the change, or at least is prepared to . . .

BRIAN WALDEN:
Like mad they did, they cheered . . .

SIR GEOFFREY HOWE:
. . . is prepared to endorse it . . .

BRIAN WALDEN:
By the way, why do you think they cheered their heads off? What do you think they were telling you?

SIR GEOFFREY HOWE:
I suspect a whole combination of emotions: affection, support, sympathy, welcome, welcome back, I don't know. The fact is that I am there as part of . . .

BRIAN WALDEN:
You might not think a bit of counter weight in that, you know . . . Geoff will hold their arm a bit?

SIR GEOFFREY HOWE:
Brian, Brian, Brian, I am there as part of that team. I'm concerned as I say, like all of us, to be sure we have the policies as well-shaped as they can be to carry them through the rest of this Parliament. I'm concerned that we sustain the revolution we've set in hand, and that involves a continuing commitment to the central disciplines: success against inflation, success in controlling public expenditure, not throwing it all away, and spreading the fruits of the revolution more widely. Now, all that is common ground between Margaret Thatcher, myself and all of us in Cabinet. There'll be discussions as to how we do it, how we sell it . . . I, I . . .

BRIAN WALDEN:
Arguments?

SIR GEOFFREY HOWE:
Sorry?

BRIAN WALDEN:
Arguments?

SIR GEOFFREY HOWE:
Of course, no doubt, yes. And I think that the feature that I also hope I bring to the presentation and preparation of government policy, is a belief that if you're going to sustain this in the long term, then you need to secure, not the enthusiastic endorsement by the entire population of what you are doing, but something more than reluctant acquiescence.

And I think one of the successes of the government is to have carried through, for example, the huge reform of industrial relations law. Again, we crossed swords in the House under the Heath government, and we failed then to sustain that. This government has sustained it because we have expanded it and taken it stage by stage.

BRIAN WALDEN:
Quite so. Can I put this to you, though? I remain marginally sceptical – though of course I'm always prepared to take your word for almost anything, Sir Geoffrey – but I'm marginally sceptical that the Prime Minister, if she's not tucking into the roast beef and yorkshire pudding, is actually watching this, is bouncing up and down with joy at the thought of having this deeply active, robust Deputy Prime Minister. I recall when John Biffen once came on one of my programmes and said some things about a balanced ticket and all that, and the next day Bernard Ingham read the death sentence. And he was dropped after the following election. Is it that you can afford to say these sort of things, because in the back of your mind, like some of the commentators, you now regard yourself as quite unsackable; that she can't get rid of you – if she doesn't like it, she's going to have to lump it, because the Conservative Party will never wear you being dismissed? Isn't that true?

SIR GEOFFREY HOWE:
I'm not in the position of analysing these matters in that kind of way, Brian.

BRIAN WALDEN:
Ah ha . . . but you think it, don't you?

SIR GEOFFREY HOWE:
And least of all discussing them in public in that kind of way. But the fact is that, as a result of recent changes, I have now been given a new job and a new role as, I hope, part of a continuing role in the success of what we've been trying to do together. I think that's widely recognised and I have no reason to doubt that the Prime Minister shares that view of the future. We've done a tremendous amount, starting from very very modest beginnings our little revolution that started fifteen years back.

BRIAN WALDEN:
Sir Geoffrey, why haven't you used the normal formula? Why haven't you said to me: "Of course I can be sacked at any moment, my job is entirely in the Prime Minister's hands"? Is it because it isn't, and you know you can't be sacked like that?

SIR GEOFFREY HOWE:
Constitutionally, the position is exactly the same, Brian . . .

BRIAN WALDEN:
Of course, but the reality is that you can't be, isn't it?

SIR GEOFFREY HOWE:
. . . exactly the same as it ever has been. But the fact is that nobody is contemplating that kind of change . . . what we're contemplating is the sustained success of what we've achieved, and the Prime Minister and I and all our colleagues have that as the overriding objective.

BRIAN WALDEN:
A last question, Sir Geoffrey. In view of all this, you haven't given up, have you, the honourable ambition of one day leading the Tory Party?

SIR GEOFFREY HOWE:
I think there is nobody who comes into politics who doesn't cherish that ambition, as I've said before, like a Field Marshall's baton in the knapsack. There are plenty of people in the present Cabinet who could assume the leadership of the Conservative Party if that were to be . . .

BRIAN WALDEN:
So the answer's, yes.

SIR GEOFFREY HOWE:
It . . . of course it's an option, but the option is not . . .

BRIAN WALDEN:
Is yes.

SIR GEOFFREY HOWE:
. . . is not available.

BRIAN WALDEN:
Sir Geoffrey, thank you very much indeed.

29TH OCTOBER, 1989

BRIAN WALDEN INTERVIEWS MARGARET THATCHER

BRIAN WALDEN:
Nigel Lawson's shock resignation from the Chancellorship has plunged the Prime Minister into the most serious political crisis of her career. It has also confronted her with a full scale economic crisis. Can she resolve her political and economic problems? The Prime Minister is with me here today.

Prime Minister, many people including many of your own supporters blame you for the resignation of Nigel Lawson from the Chancellorship, and he blames you. This is what he wrote: "Dear Margaret, the successful conduct of economic policy is possible only if there is, and is seen to be, full agreement between the Prime Minister and the Chancellor of the Exchequer. Recent events have confirmed that this essential requirement cannot be satisfied so long as Alan Walters remains your personal economic adviser. I have therefore regretfully concluded that it is in the best interests of the Government for me to resign my office without further ado." Now Prime Minister, how you respond to this claim of blame may be of crucial significance for you personally and for your government. So I put it to you, are you to blame for Nigel Lawson's resignation?

MARGARET THATCHER:
Well, we have done very well together for the last six years and very well for Britain, and I think the results are clear to see. To me the Chancellor's position was unassailable. I always supported him and said quite clearly, "advisers are there to advise, ministers are there to decide", and that was the way we did business and we did it very successfully. I tried very hard to dissuade the Chancellor from going, but he had made up his mind and in the end I had to accept his resignation and appoint someone else.

BRIAN WALDEN:
Let's look though at what he says, you see . . . he is making the claim

here that successful conduct of economic policy is possible only if there is seen to be full agreement between the Prime Minister and the Chancellor of the Exchequer. Now he's right about that, isn't he?

MARGARET THATCHER:
Yes, and I am right about the successful six years he's had in the Treasury – very successful, the economy of Britain has made great strides under his Chancellorship and we have worked together. Those are the facts . . .

BRIAN WALDEN:
But you . . .

MARGARET THATCHER:
. . . and no-one can get round them, it has been extremely successful.

BRIAN WALDEN:
But you're not claiming, Prime Minister – it may or may not have been extremely successful – but you're not claiming that there was seen to be full agreement between yourself and the Chancellor, are you?

MARGARET THATCHER:
I am claiming that I fully backed and supported the Chancellor. Of course we discuss things, we discuss things in Cabinet, we discuss things in the Economic Committee, we discuss things with many advisers. There's not only one adviser, there are many advisers in the Treasury, we have many advisers, and we hammered out a policy and on that policy we were totally agreed, totally, and it was implemented, and it was implemented very successfully and the success matters.

BRIAN WALDEN:
That may or it may not – I mean, many Conservatives would agree with you – I suppose the Opposition wouldn't – that may or may not be true, but I must press you again, Prime Minister, plainly he – Lawson – didn't think that you were *seen* to agree, else he wouldn't have resigned. He *did* resign.

MARGARET THATCHER:
He heard me say many many times faced with this question: "I fully support my Chancellor" – and of course you do. We could not have been successful if I hadn't, and I did, and we worked out many many things together . . .

BRIAN WALDEN:
All right, Prime Minister . . .

MARGARET THATCHER:
Advisers advise, ministers decide. Nigel was decisive, I was decisive . . . the result was success.

BRIAN WALDEN:
OK, but it's pretty obvious from the letter what it is he objects to. He objects to the position of . . . as he then held . . . of Professor Alan Walters, and he says: "This essential requirement cannot be satisfied so long as Alan Walters remains your personal economic adviser." Now he must have made that clear to you, what did you say to that?

MARGARET THATCHER:
Nigel's position, as I said to him, is unassailable. He was a very strong Chancellor . . .

BRIAN WALDEN:
It isn't now, is it? He's gone.

MARGARET THATCHER
This is his choice. I tried to persuade him to stay. I couldn't believe that he would go when he's been such a strong Chancellor, and his position *was* unassailable. And he knows and I know that the adviser's role is to put his view, the minister's role is to take a lot of advice, to discuss things, to analyse them, to work them out, to consider the political problems which arise, and then to decide. We did just that. Somehow Nigel had made up his mind that he was going. I spent a long time just talking, just the two of us together, trying to dissuade him, but his mind was made up. I was sad but then once he had decided to go then one had to accept it and set about refashioning one's Cabinet.

BRIAN WALDEN:
But Prime Minister, it's fairly clear, isn't it, what was getting up Nigel's nose? It wasn't that you had an economic adviser who very quietly and silently whispered things to you in the still watches of the night. He felt that it . . . you weren't seen to be united because Professor Alan Walters, a very able man, was making absolutely clear, to anybody who cared to listen to him, fundamental disagreements that he had with the Chancellor, and Nigel feared that people would therefore assume that these were *your* views and that's what he means when he says you weren't seen to be united. Now surely he put that point to you, and what did you say to that?

MARGARET THATCHER:
Alan Walters is part-time as my adviser. He's only just recently returned. The article to which you're referring was written over a year ago. It is just not possible that this small particular thing could result in this

particular resignation. You know full well that the press have been causing trouble for a very long time, no matter how much, no matter how firmly I have supported Nigel, no matter how firmly we have been saying the same things – that I'm afraid was a fact of life, that was what they were doing. It's not for me to say how they saw it, it is for me to say that Nigel has advisers, that I had Alan Walters part-time – there only a few days a month – that Nigel and I and others hammered out the economic policy. We did so successfully. Neither of us is manipulated in any way by advisers, neither of us thinks that we knew everything, that we didn't have to take advice. We did, we listened to it, we decided, we succeeded, and I am very sad that he's gone. But he has and now we must turn to the future, the same policies will continue because they are sound and we shall carry on in precisely the same way.

BRIAN WALDEN:
Oh, I want to ask you about that of course, Prime Minister. But let's come back to Professor Alan Walters. You see, it isn't just this article that he wrote 15 months ago and that got recent publicity, it's very well known – and you must know it – that Professor Alan Walters has been going round the City, he's been attending lunches, he's been giving journalists his views on matters and he's been expressing disagreements with Lawson. Lawson wouldn't just have objected about an ancient article, what he objected is the whole basis of Alan Walters' activities. Now, isn't that the case?

MARGARET THATCHER:
Many people in departments, at the top of Civil Service departments, go out and have lunches in the City. They have to keep in contact, particularly if they're in economic departments, that is not unknown at all. But Brian, I'm not going to get involved in this tittle-tattle. I've had a very competent adviser. Nigel also had very competent advisers. They worked together, Alan and his advisers. I'm not going to get involved in this. There are far bigger things to consider. The economy has been run extremely successfully. We've created more wealth than ever before, and spread it more widely than ever before, a standard of living people have never had before, and a reputation of Britain overseas that is second to none. These are the achievements and I'm not concerned with the tittle-tattle. I'm concerned with getting on with the job, and that I shall do.

BRIAN WALDEN:
Well, Prime Minister, I couldn't agree with you more about tittle-tattle and as you well know I have nothing to do with it myself. But this is not tittle-tattle. For instance, look at what Sam Brittan said in the *Financial Times* yesterday – their most distinguished correspondent and Assistant Editor: "There is one thing on which I will stake my reputation, this is that the constant flow of rumours and speculation about Thatcher . . .

Thatcher and Walters . . . was undermining the pound, the British economy and the prospects of job increases." Now, that's what Lawson objected to – why didn't you, when he asked you to, sack Alan Walters?

MARGARET THATCHER:
I am not responsible for rumours. I see many things in the press that are totally and utterly false, totally and utterly false, they're speculation, I'm not responsible for those. I am responsible for the conduct of business. Nigel and I worked very well together with great success. Now, let's consider the policy.

BRIAN WALDEN:
All right, well . . . let's consider *Lawson.* I mean I have to take it the way you have put it, Prime Minister, that you blame Nigel for the resignation, not yourself.

MARGARET THATCHER:
It is not a question of blaming anyone. Nigel was a very successful . . . brilliantly successful Chancellor for six years. Of course I knew that one day he would go. He's an extremely able person and I knew that one day we would lose him. I didn't expect it to happen this way or as soon as I've said to you. To me Nigel's position was unassailable and I supported him wholeheartedly. He decided to go. Now, that is a fact and I have appointed a new Chancellor whose ambition it was to be Chancellor, a new Home Secretary whose ambition it was to be Home Secretary, a new Foreign Secretary whose ambition it was to be Foreign Secretary. Now let's get on with the future. We've had a very successful past. That chapter has come to an end. I'm sorry it did, but it is the future now that matters.

BRIAN WALDEN:
It is, but it is also of course your political position, Prime Minister, and I have to question you on that. And you know that I do . . .

MARGARET THATCHER:
Yes, do go question . . . go ahead.

BRIAN WALDEN:
Of course. Now . . . so let me ask you again: *Why* did Nigel resign? You say he knew that he was unassailable, he knew that you loved him and that everything he did was marvellous, but he *resigned.* Now people are going to want to know, why?

MARGARET THATCHER:
I think that is a question you must put to him and not to me. I tried to dissuade him. I saw him three times on Thursday. At first I really didn't

believe that he had any intention of going, and then just before Questions he told me that he would be going and I said: "Look, I must go to Questions and deal with the House and the statement, I will see you immediately I return and perhaps we can talk it through" . . . and so we talked it through just the two of us and it was quite clear that he *had* made up his mind and there was nothing I could do to dissuade him . . . quite clear. It was . . . that was just a fact of life and I had to accept it. More you must ask of him. He went with great dignity . . .

BRIAN WALDEN:
He's coming on next week . . .

MARGARET THATCHER:
He's been . . .

BRIAN WALDEN:
. . . so I'll have the chance.

MARGARET THATCHER:
. . . he's been very generous in the remarks he's made about John Major and very supportive, and he will continue to be supportive as you would expect of him.

BRIAN WALDEN:
Well you see, again, Prime Minister, obviously you saw Nigel several times on that Thursday, four times was it?

MARGARET THATCHER:
I saw him just before we . . . just before 9 o'clock. I had seen him the previous day on our regular bilateral meeting. Then of course we had Cabinet, then I saw him . . . he wanted to see me just before I went in to Questions, and then after Questions. The long discussion was, of course, after Questions.

BRIAN WALDEN:
All right, Prime Minister, but I have to put it back to you, and you know that I do, because everybody is going to ask you about this again and again. He was unassailable, you say, you were in agreement, you say, everything was going well, you say, and he said to you, "Margaret, you have got to get rid of Alan Walters." Why didn't you, and keep your Chancellor?

MARGARET THATCHER:
Nigel had determined to go. I made it quite clear that advisers are there to give advice, ministers are there to decide. You have asked me, Brian, the same question about five times, and I have given you the same

answer. If you continue to ask that same question, I shall continue to give you the same answer. I am concerned now with future policy and with the conduct of it, and with the future Chancellor of the Exchequer, and the conduct of the Economic Policy Committee of the Cabinet, and the Cabinet, and in the House of Commons. I'm answerable for that. Nigel made his decision – reluctantly I accepted it.

BRIAN WALDEN:
I want to come on to future policy but I also want to clear this up, which will not just go away. A last question: do you deny that Nigel would have stayed if you had sacked Professor Alan Walters?

MARGARET THATCHER:
I don't know. I don't know.

BRIAN WALDEN:
You never even thought to ask him that?

MARGARET THATCHER:
I . . . that is not . . . I don't know. Nigel had determined that he was going to put in his resignation, I did everything possible to stop him.

BRIAN WALDEN:
But . . .

MARGARET THATCHER:
I was not successful. No, you're going on asking the same question . . .

BRIAN WALDEN:
Of course, but that's a terrible admission, Prime Minister.

MARGARET THATCHER:
I have nothing further . . . I don't know . . . of course I don't know.

BRIAN WALDEN:
You don't know, you could have kept your Chancellor, possibly, if you had sacked your part-time adviser?

MARGARET THATCHER:
I wanted to keep my Chancellor in any event, because he was very good, his position was unassailable, and let's face it, Brian, he *was* Chancellor. He and I decided. This is not a matter of advisers. Nigel and I and the Economic Committee *decided.* We answer to the House of Commons. Now *that* is the fact and that is the big fact of the matter, and I'm not going on with this.

BRIAN WALDEN:
All right, we . . . I think have in some ways got fairly clearly . . . I suppose I must ask you once more, just once more, did . . . you say you don't know whether you could have kept him if Walters had gone . . . did he ask you to sack Walters?

MARGARET THATCHER:
I'm not going to disclose the conversations which the two of us had together . . .

BRIAN WALDEN:
All right. All right.

MARGARET THATCHER:
. . . I admired Nigel very much. I'm immensely grateful for his stewardship as Chancellor. Nigel was Chancellor. Nigel's position was unassailable. Unassailable.

BRIAN WALDEN:
I can't make you say, Prime Minister, what you don't want to say, but of course you are aware what people will assume from this discussion, don't you; that you *could* have kept the Chancellor if you had sacked Walters.

MARGARET THATCHER:
I wanted to keep Nigel. The position of the Chancellor is a very great one, it does not depend upon advisers at all. Mine doesn't depend upon advisers. I make the decisions, Nigel makes the decisions, we discuss those together. That is the important fact and I think people will see it as that. Advisers – many of them – are there to advise, ministers to decide. Nigel made his decision, I had to accept it.

BRIAN WALDEN:
All right, let's look at it from the other point of view now, Prime Minister. This is not something that suddenly blew up. It's been known, in pretty well all circles, and indeed it's one of the reasons that there has been trouble in the markets, that there *have* been disagreements between yourself and the Chancellor.

MARGARET THATCHER:
There have *not* been many troubles in the markets . . . of course markets are there . . .

BRIAN WALDEN:
And no disagreements between yourself and the Chancellor?

MARGARET THATCHER:
Of course markets go up and down, you wouldn't have a market if it didn't. What do you mean trouble in the markets?

BRIAN WALDEN:
Oh, because, well, the Sam Brittan quote . . .

MARGARET THATCHER:
There was a Stock Exchange crash in 1987.

BRIAN WALDEN:
Oh sure, I don't mean that.

MARGARET THATCHER:
There was trouble on Wall Street when it fell just 150 points and my goodness me, all television and radio and the press tried to blow it up as big as they could – that is the way they work. The markets were far calmer than either television or the press, and the markets have been far calmer. Now let's start the question again in a different way.

BRIAN WALDEN:
Well, all right, I will, I will. If you won't take *my* word for it that there's been trouble in the markets, and of course I didn't mean the Stock Exchange crash, let me read you the first paragraph of the leader in the *Financial Times* yesterday, and it says: "With his resignation yesterday Mr Lawson put an end at last to what has long been an impossible situation, both for him personally and for the government as well. It is more than likely that the behaviour of the Prime Minister which drove him from office may be seen in hindsight as the beginning of the end for her, too." An impossible situation. All the financial journalists are saying that there was enormous uncertainty in the markets because of the presumed disagreement between you and the Chancellor. Now, do you deny that?

MARGARET THATCHER:
Brian, you must be quite crazy. Do you think that kind of situation could have gone on for six years? Alan Walters was . . .

BRIAN WALDEN:
Could have for eighteen months though, couldn't it?

MARGARET THATCHER:
Do you really think that kind of situation could have gone on for six years?

BRIAN WALDEN:
Yes, everybody thinks that . . .

MARGARET THATCHER:
One moment . . .

BRIAN WALDEN:
Eighteen months

MARGARET THATCHER:
No, they do not . . .

BRIAN WALDEN:
Eighteen months . . .

MARGARET THATCHER:
Oh well, you've come from six years to eighteen months, pretty smartly.

BRIAN WALDEN:
Yes . . .

MARGARET THATCHER:
Let's get it down to eighteen days, or eighteen minutes, or eighteen seconds!

BRIAN WALDEN:
Eighteen months is a long time.

MARGARET THATCHER:
Look, Brian, we had six years of highly successful stewardship from the Chancellor of the Exchequer, six years, very successful, created more wealth and spread it more around than ever before: better social services, higher standard of living, high reputation abroad. If you think that could have gone on for six years with that success you're talking nonsense. Now let's stop this simple tittle-tattle. Let's get down to the success we've had, the way in which people now copy Thatcherism, as they call it, the world over; the proud reputation we have abroad, the way people listen to us – we couldn't have had all of that unless Nigel and I had worked *very* closely together. We did. Now let's go on to the future.

BRIAN WALDEN:
Well it isn't tittle-tattle.

MARGARET THATCHER:
Don't you want to face the future?

BRIAN WALDEN:
Of course I do . . . I'm . . .

MARGARET THATCHER:
I do, and I'm ready to face it.

BRIAN WALDEN:
I'm most anxious to talk about the future, Prime Minister . . .

MARGARET THATCHER:
Good . . .

BRIAN WALDEN:
. . . but I'm, also anxious to talk about the political aspects of this crisis.

MARGARET THATCHER:
Yes.

BRIAN WALDEN:
And there are, you know there are. You see, there *have been* disagreements between you and Lawson in the last eighteen months, he says so himself. Now . . . and they have caused certain uncertainties on the market. The question I want to put to you is this: if you found that you could not resolve these things in private with him, rather than lose Alan Walters why didn't you sack Lawson and appoint a new Chancellor?

MARGARET THATCHER:
We have resolved them. I think you're probably talking about the European aspect and Exchange Rate Mechanism, we resolved that and we set it out at Madrid – precisely what we intended to do and how we intended to go in the future – and we have adhered to it absolutely because we hammered it out.

BRIAN WALDEN:
Let me switch from Lawson, keeping on this issue of the political problems that you face, to something that some people say – you may want to accept it, you may want to reject it – but some people draw a lesson from all this. They say it isn't the first time. Margaret Thatcher has problems with strong independent figures, look at Heseltine at the time of Westland, look at Biffen whom she got rid of, look at even Sir Geoffrey Howe who had to be moved from the Foreign Office in rather unhappy circumstances and all that, she just cannot get on with anybody except yes-men. Now is that true, Prime Minister?

MARGARET THATCHER:
No, and it is a great insult to members of my Cabinet and you know it. You also know from many many years of arguing with me that I enjoy a good argument.

BRIAN WALDEN:
I know.

MARGARET THATCHER:
I enjoy dealing with the facts. We conduct affairs so that we do have very good arguments about things because that's the way we come to conclusions. I like strong men and strong women about me, that way we have strong government. I have nothing like the problems which the Labour Party has. We have strong policies founded on strong principles and a record of success and an international reputation, and country after country following our policies as they come in and say to me: "We've tried everything else, now we'll try Thatcherism." And I say to them, Thatcherism is much older than me. It's based on fundamental common sense, the limitation of the powers of government and handing more and more powers and the fruits of their work back to people. And it works . . .

BRIAN WALDEN:
All right.

MARGARET THATCHER:
That's what matters. Yes, I like strong people about me, yes I'm prepared to argue *anything,* yes I'm prepared to listen. Why? Because I want the result to be *right.* I want the policy to be *right.* I want to have all the arguments put, because if they're not put to me at Number 10 and we don't argue them out, they'll be put to me in the House of Commons and I'm able to face them in the House of Commons because we have thrashed them all out in Number 10. So what you're saying again is nonsense, and you know it from having talked with me over the years.

BRIAN WALDEN:
All right, now I'll come back to that because I think there's a very vital point involved there which I really want to put to you, but let me sum you up so far. You do *not* accept blame for the resignation of the Chancellor of the Exchequer, you don't know why he resigned. He is to tell me himself. You can offer no guidance on that. And you *don't* accept that the other resignations from your government or the other sackings from your government have arisen because you can't handle strong men, because you like strong men and you like arguing with them. Let me put this to you, Prime Minister. It's a point that's always interested me, and I think it's now politically relevant. It may be the case that in private you will have a lusty argument and you will listen to other people's opinions and that you're only too happy to accept a suggestion if it's correct, but you never come over *in public* like that, *ever.* You come over as being someone who one of your backbenchers said is slightly off her trolley, authoritarian, domineering, refusing to listen to anybody else – why? Why cannot you publicly project what you have just told me is your private character?

MARGARET THATCHER:
Brian, if anyone's coming over as domineering in this interview it's you. It's you.

BRIAN WALDEN:
You think so?

MARGARET THATCHER:
Hammering things out instead of just talking them in a conversational way. Yes, you're very domineering at the moment. Now let's deal with the authoritarian thing quietly. No government has handed back more powers to the people than this one, the one I have the privilege to lead. Taxation: we've lowered the levels of income tax – that is more power to people over their own money and earnings; that I believe in because of incentives, people work for their families – so have handed power back, we take less, they have more. We have cut some of the controls which government used to use to control the economy: incomes controls, prices controls, foreign exchange controls . . . a development certificate, so factories used to have to get a development as well as a planning certificate, so that they had to be told to develop where they didn't want to, and not where they wanted to, and that led to trouble . . . that's gone. A lot of controls have gone. We used to have masses of nationalised industries – let me give you steel as an example. It was losing a billion a year which had to be met by the tax-payer. It's now privatised making a profit of 500 million a year. We've privatised industry after industry. Government ought not to control business, it doesn't know how to do it, it interferes. So in all of those things . . . and in home ownership we've taken more power away from councils and let people buy their own houses . . . in all of these things, and now in the reform of the health service, in the reforms of education, less powers to government and local government and more powers to the people. The whole *characteristic* of the government which I lead has been to limit the powers of government, to be very strong on those things which only government can do, very strong, and to hand over powers to people. This is the British character: it's enterprising, it's responsible, it will take the initiative, it wants to look after its own family, wants to make its own decisions. Authoritarian? It is *socialism* that is authoritarian, it is *socialism* that says you must conform to the national plan, to the government. I am totally different. Government is there to serve . . .

BRIAN WALDEN:
All right, Prime Minister.

MARGARET THATCHER:
. . . the freedom of the people under a strong rule of law. We have handed powers back to the people, checked the power of government,

enlarged the powers, the liberties, the income, the ownership of property, the choice of the people. It is the reverse . . . what you are saying is the reverse.

BRIAN WALDEN:
Well actually, I wasn't necessarily denying any of that, it may be true, it may not be true. I thought since you thought I was domineering you, I ought to let you say a lot of it. But you know what it is that I'm getting at. You see, you accept, in public, no blame for anything that has happened with Lawson and indeed not much blame for anything else – why? Don't you think that it would be truer to your own nature if you said in front of the public – who don't think that you're weak or lack conviction, that's not what they're afraid of; the reason they might not vote for you is that they think you've got *too* much conviction, that you're *too* dogmatic, that you won't listen to *anybody* – why don't you say: "Well, all right, I had a quarrel with Nigel, perhaps there were faults on both sides, I do take a little bit of blame, I should have been more sensitive to his worry about Walters" . . . why don't you say that?

MARGARET THATCHER:
Well, neither of us is faultless, none of us is claiming that. Of course we have faults, of course I take the blame for most things that go wrong, now and then a little credit for things which go right. That's life, what's the problem?

BRIAN WALDEN:
Ah, well then what *was* the blame that you are prepared to accept for losing Nigel?

MARGARET THATCHER:
Nigel had decided to go, I tried to keep him . . .

BRIAN WALDEN:
So you *don't* accept blame?

MARGARET THATCHER:
. . . and I would still try to keep him, I would still try to keep him, but he decided to go and I had to make my decisions from that time. Nigel made his, I made mine. The idea, you know, that you can have the same government for ten years, you know, is totally untenable. You wouldn't have your young people staying, they've got to see that their ambitions may be fulfilled and rise from the bottom to the top. You know full well one has to have reshuffles, and I've had quite a number. The reasons for resignations in the past have been totally different and Michael Heseltine could not accept the collective decision of Cabinet. You have to.

BRIAN WALDEN:
All right.

MARGARET THATCHER:
But we have had several reshuffles. I regret this resignation, it has happened, we shall go forward and as I indicated yesterday it will be business as usual. Nigel is a loss. He will support this government vigorously as I have supported him.

BRIAN WALDEN:
I can almost feel the desire to accept some measure of blame trembling on your lips but it can't quite come out and as you rightly say we must get onto the future, there . . .

MARGARET THATCHER:
Yes, because you're . . .

BRIAN WALDEN:
. . . there are economic problems involved in this.

MARGARET THATCHER:
. . . yes you're having a highly artificial argument. Let's get on to the realities.

BRIAN WALDEN:
Well no, it's the one the country wants to hear about, it's the political argument, but after the break . . .

MARGARET THATCHER:
No, no, you're not having the political argument, you are having tittle-tattle argument, now let's get on to the political argument.

BRIAN WALDEN:
Prime Minister, it's not tittle-tattle. I can assure you that when you get down to the House of Commons next week you will hear very little else. However, I want to come onto the economic argument, but we must for the moment take a break.

. . . .

BRIAN WALDEN:
Prime Minister, let us now switch to the economic side of all this, because one of the unfortunate aspects of Lawson going is that it has, if anything, deepened the confusion about your intentions, and I know you want to clear these up. Now, you mentioned earlier about the Madrid

Summit. One of the problems with that is that practically everybody thinks that the wording adopted there was a fudge that both you and Nigel can stand on, though you actually intended different things. Similarly, every government minister now says the policies will go on just as they were before – and I'm sure they will – but that doesn't help much because the markets have felt that there was a division there anyway. So I want to put it to you what is really, I suppose, the essential question that the markets will want to hear: do you really want to join the European Exchange Rate Mechanism of the European Monetary System?

MARGARET THATCHER:
We shall join the European Monetary System on the conditions we laid down in Madrid. There was nothing fudged about them, they were quite clear. Point number one: the various countries in that particular exchange rate play by different rules. That is nonsense. When you join any system, you must all play by the same rules. At the moment, some have a foreign exchange control, some don't; some have freer movement of capital, some don't; some have artificial constraints on what their pension funds and insurance funds can invest in which prevent overseas investment or investment in other currencies, some don't; some have a great deal of subsidy to their industry so that competition is unfair, some don't. You just simply can't have a system with a currency like sterling, which is a big currency, which is a more open currency, which has London as the most open market, freest market in the world, playing under that higgledy-piggledy set of rules. We're way ahead of most other countries in our liberty, in our freedom, in our openness. They have to catch up with us. I hope they will, and so we said quite clearly we shall join the exchange rate system when there are no foreign exchange controls, when there's freedom of movement of capital, when their financial services like their insurance and pension funds are run as openly and as freely as ours are and when we have fair competition and the subsidies have gone. Now, all of that should happen during the first stage – what is called the Delors first stage – the first stage coming towards monetary union. I hope it will, but other countries have to catch up a long way before it happens. How long it will take is up to them. France says that she will get rid of her foreign exchange controls, I think by July next year. I'm not sure about Italy or Spain. I think they might want longer. And then we'll see . . .

BRIAN WALDEN:
They've got till '92, Spain and Ireland have . . .

MARGARET THATCHER:
Yes, and then you will see whether . . .

BRIAN WALDEN:
. . . Greece and Portugal till '94.

MARGARET THATCHER:
Yes, well, Portugal's a much smaller currency . . . and then we'll see whether the exchange rate can hold under those circumstances. I hope it does but *they* have to catch up with *us*.

BRIAN WALDEN:
Shall I tell you what I suspect, not from my point of view but from yours, Prime Minister, might be the trouble with that answer? It's very clear, it's very logical and you've always said it. But especially now Lawson's gone there's a slight smell of hostility to the ERM about it. If you could show some *enthusiasm* for wanting to get in you might cheer the markets up. Are you enthusiastic to get in?

MARGARET THATCHER:
I have just indicated I hope that the other countries will catch us up in free liberalised markets, free movement of capital which is in the Treaty of Rome and we're one of the first countries to have it, Germany has it, Holland has it. I hope they will catch us up. When they do in all those particulars and we have free movement, when we have genuine competition, when they get rid of some of their hidden restraints . . .

BRIAN WALDEN:
All right . . .

MARGARET THATCHER:
. . . and they have them . . . and when they're prepared to abide by the rules as we do and I hope they do.

BRIAN WALDEN:
Well, which way is it in your mind, Prime Minister: that you are thinking, "I'm dying to get into this because it will be very good for the pound and it will be very good for Britain. I do wish these foolish foreigners would hurry up and get into a situation where I can join," or are you privately thinking, "I don't reckon these chaps will ever in the near future get around to doing any of these things, so I'm quite all right, we shall never have to join the ERM which I don't want to join anyway"? Which it . . . which is it?

MARGARET THATCHER:
I hope they will, and I hope it not only for the Exchange Rate Mechanism so that we can join, but I hope it on general economic grounds. We believe in an open economy, we believe in free and fair trade, we believe in fair competition, but *they* have some artifical and cultural barriers

which are going to be very difficult to get down. *They* talk about being European and communitaire, *we* practise it. We're much more open than they are and they really have to start to do things as well as say them. It's no earthly good talking about these things unless they're prepared to free up . . . the more they free up the better pleased I shall be . . .

BRIAN WALDEN:
Ah . . .

MARGARET THATCHER:
. . . but they must expect to play fairly. We wanted . . . we joined the European Community for the Common Market. It's one of the things we haven't had. They've had their barriers up and they still, many of them, have their barriers up. There are still some of them which, no matter how in theory you free up contracts, will always buy German or always will buy French whereas we look at value for money. But I really can't have Britain worsted by other people having a different set of rules from the ones we have. We play fair and we will, and the more liberal economics they have, using it with a small 'l', the better it will please me and I shall be delighted when they have it.

BRIAN WALDEN:
All right, Prime Minister, but I still detect a certain underlying suspicion of these people, a certain hostility to what they're up to, a certain feeling that yes, they . . . they've got a lot to change and they must mend their ways in many ways, and you won't go in until they do, will you?

MARGARET THATCHER:
Because it would not be fair to Britain . . .

BRIAN WALDEN:
All right.

MARGARET THATCHER:
. . . it would not be fair to Britain. Just take one example where we have really to bat extremely hard. There are more small farms in Germany and France than there are in Britain, and they want to fix the Common Agricultural Policy so that it always favours their smaller farms and puts bigger family farms at risk. It is quite absurd, and we have to fight like tigers for our bigger family farms. It's not fair, and of course I fight for Britain, and of course I'm combative, and of course I fought for Britain over . . . over the . . . the Common Agricultural Policy and I shall go on doing it, but they simply must be fair.

BRIAN WALDEN:
All right, Prime Minister, but on the basis of putting *that* to me, there's

a lot that they've got to get rid of. What it means in practice is that we shan't be going into the ERM for quite some time, doesn't it?

MARGARET THATCHER:
That depends on them. That depends on the gap between what they say and what they do.

BRIAN WALDEN:
I think, don't you, Prime Minister, that the markets are bound to interpret this to mean that you have no especial enthusiasm for getting into the ERM as it is . . .

MARGARET THATCHER:
No, Brian . . .

BRIAN WALDEN:
. . . and you're rather doubtful how long it's going to take them to get into a position where you can get in?

MARGARET THATCHER:
No, Brian.

BRIAN WALDEN:
You don't think the markets will think that?

MARGARET THATCHER:
No, and I think you're trying to persuade them artificially into a way which is not justified from what I have just said, and that is one of the problems we deal with. Let the markets make their own judgment. We shall go in when it is fair – and under the same rules and under liberal economics – to do so, and that, Brian, is what the Common Market is all about.

BRIAN WALDEN:
Well, was supposed to be about . . .

MARGARET THATCHER:
It's not keeping . . . that's right . . . it's not keeping constraints, it's genuinely getting them down within the Common Market as an example to others, and I repeat it, we are ahead of others and I hope they catch up. We are far more communitaire in the way in which we run our trade and run our finance . . .

BRIAN WALDEN:
All right . . .

MARGARET THATCHER:
. . . and I hope they'll catch up so that we can join and have . . . er . . . join the Exchange Rate Mechanism.

BRIAN WALDEN:
Don't sound very sure about it?

MARGARET THATCHER:
It's a terrible title, isn't it?

BRIAN WALDEN:
It is . . . awful . . .

MARGARET THATCHER:
Exchange Rate Mechanism.

BRIAN WALDEN:
And you don't sound very sure about it either, do you?

MARGARET THATCHER:
I am very sure about it.

BRIAN WALDEN:
Oh no no no, that they will catch up.

MARGARET THATCHER:
I am very sure about it.

BRIAN WALDEN:
That they will catch up is what I meant.

MARGARET THATCHER:
Well, I hope they will.

BRIAN WALDEN:
Let me knock off Greece and Portugal because this is a point that's been put to me several times and the answers are unclear, because there's some claim that the Treasury said one thing and you said another, but I shan't pursue that.

MARGARET THATCHER:
Well, they'll claim that in any case.

BRIAN WALDEN:
Of course, and they may well be, they may be right.

MARGARET THATCHER:
We could have the identical words and you would claim . . .

BRIAN WALDEN:
Been known to happen. Well, let me ask you on detail . . . Greece and Portugal have got until July '94, 1994, to get rid of their exchange controls.

MARGARET THATCHER:
Well, you would expect that. Portugal is a much poorer country, she must have . . .

BRIAN WALDEN:
So . . . so that doesn't worry you?

MARGARET THATCHER:
She must have. It's reasonable to have a transition period always . . .

BRIAN WALDEN:
And that wouldn't keep you out?

MARGARET THATCHER:
No, it's reasonable for them, because they're much smaller currencies. We are a much bigger currency, a bigger currency than any other except the Deutschmark and therefore for us to go in would be much much different from Portugal.

BRIAN WALDEN:
The franc and the lira have got to get rid of exchange controls, but Greece and Portugal you're tolerant about.

MARGARET THATCHER:
Well, Dutch . . . the Holland . . . Dutch people already have got rid of their foreign exchange controls, and so has Luxembourg, so it's not necessarily the size. But Greece joined later, she's a poorer country. Portugal joined later and Portugal will still have a longer transition period and so will Spain, because she's got until 1992.

BRIAN WALDEN:
Let me ask you now about the second really crucial issue, the only other one that basically matters in terms of market confidence, and that's the value of the pound. Nigel persistently, as you know, interfered with interest rates in order to keep sterling within certain bounds, in order to support it when it fell and sometimes to depress it when it rose. Is that policy going to be pursued?

MARGARGET THATCHER:
I like a strong pound. Most Chancellors and most Prime Ministers *like* a strong pound. You have markets where the pound goes up and down, and don't forget the Exchange Rate Mechanism applies only to European currencies, most of the world's trade is conducted in the dollar and the yen and you have . . . you will have currencies going up and down against the dollar and the yen, and joining the ERM won't affect that. You have really only two mechanisms, that is. One is the interest rates and the other is intervention, and don't think that going into the Exchange Rate Mechanism is an easy option. You could have to swing up your interest rates extremely sharply because you had no option because you're in a fixed particular bracket. So . . .

BRIAN WALDEN:
Sure, but I am talking about domestic interest rates, and what I'm really putting to you is if the markets get very jittery next week – and who knows, they often do – will you then, in fact, use interest rates in order to keep the value of the pound up?

MARGARET THATCHER:
You manage the markets on a day-to-day basis, and you make your decisions, and if ever you reveal what your decisions are likely to be you're only helping the speculators. That I will not do, and you would not expect me to do.

BRIAN WALDEN:
No.

MARGARET THATCHER:
I like a strong pound. There are only two ways: one is the interest rate, the other is intervention, and the other is I think the general demeanour and politics and stability of the Government. We've had a strong economy, we continue to have a strong economy. We have a strong government and we have a good majority, and I hope they'll make their judgement of Britain's strong economy, and also may I say its strong leadership, and of a very good team leading and a united party. And that has an effect, that has an effect. There's nothing mechanical about exchange rates.

BRIAN WALDEN:
Prime Minister, I think the impact of the whole interview . . . of course it may not – matter of opinion – you may think differently . . . will make many people feel that nothing that has happened has in any way shaken or chastened you, and of course that will worry some of them. They will say: "The Prime Minister remains absolutely unyielding about everything, and though she might have done a good job I think it's time in fact

that we had someone who was more yielding." Now, what do you say to that?

MARGARET THATCHER:
Nonsense, Brian. I'm staying my own sweet reasonable self, founded on very strong convictions, which were a combination of reason and emotion. I feel passionately about personal liberty and government's there to serve it. I feel passionately that it's the right of people to have more and more choice, because I held these passionate convictions and fashioned our economic policies on them reasonably, firmly, strongly . . .

BRIAN WALDEN:
Prime Minister, I must . . .

MARGARET THATCHER:
Britain . . . they knew what . . .

BRIAN WALDEN:
I must stop you there.

MARGARET THATCHER:
No . . . no, you must not.

BRIAN WALDEN:
I must. Thank you very much indeed.

MARGARET THATCHER:
Strong leadership will continue.

5TH NOVEMBER, 1989

BRIAN WALDEN INTERVIEWS NIGEL LAWSON

BRIAN WALDEN:
Nigel Lawson's shock resignation as Chancellor remains shrouded in confusion ten days after it happened. Last Sunday the Prime Minister told me she didn't know why he'd gone. So why exactly did he? Nigel Lawson, the former Chancellor, is with me today to give his account.

Mr Lawson, despite ten days of immense speculation and an enormous amount of comment, both on television and indeed in the press, there are still all sorts of obscurities surrounding the circumstances of your resignation. I think one of the things that puzzles people most is that last week the Prime Minister told me that she didn't know why you had resigned. Now, do you accept that in the three meetings that you had with her on that day, you did not make clear to her the nature of the difficulties that you wanted resolved?

NIGEL LAWSON:
I believe I made it perfectly clear, I have to say. After all, I've known the Prime Minister for a very long time, I worked with her for a very long time, over ten years as a minister and very nearly six-and-a-half years as Chancellor of the Exchequer, during which time we'd worked together very closely and I think we understood each other – I certainly thought we understood each other – we both of us speak our minds and I expressed myself, as I say, as clearly as I possibly could.

BRIAN WALDEN:
Let's establish what it was you spoke to her clearly about. You said subsequently that it was the position of Sir Alan Walters that was giving you concern, on the grounds that his activities seemed to point out a disagreement between yourself and the Prime Minister on the economy, and that so long as he remained in place that impression was bound to endure. Now, did you make clear to the Prime Minister that it was Sir Alan Walters' position that was worrying you?

NIGEL LAWSON:

Oh yes, indeed, when I first went to see her. I . . . I'd seen her, of course, the previous day – the day that she'd arrived back from the Commonwealth Prime Ministers' meeting at Kuala Lumpur – I'd seen her for a normal bilateral to dis . . . to update her with what was going on in the economy – there was a meeting with private secretaries present but otherwise just the two of us, as ministers – and at the end of that meeting I'd said to her that I wished to discuss with her, some other time, the Alan Walters problem. I didn't push it then . . . she had – and I explained to her when I saw her on the Thursday morning that she was exhausted on the Wednesday, she'd come back without any sleep, come back, I think, at 4 o'clock in the morning and this was something very important that I had to say to her and I didn't want to spring it on her then – so I waited till the next day when she'd had a good night's sleep. And I explained to her that so long as Alan Walters remained as her personal economic adviser, conducting himself in the way he did and indeed holding the views that he was known to hold, then my position as Chancellor – and it would have been the same for anybody else as Chancellor – was untenable; because what was happening, was that he was not just giving private advice. I know many people might think it's a bit odd resigning over something like this, after all, private advice, what, what could be that . . . what's the matter with that? But it was not just a matter of private advice. What he was doing – and it was well known, he was doing it in London, he was doing it when he went over to the United States – was giving views which were different from the Government's views, different from the . . . my views, on some of the most sensitive aspects of policy: monetary policy, which means in particular interest rates, and exchange rate policy, and the inter-action between the two. Now, those are highly market-sensitive. And when the markets hear two different voices because they think – maybe wrongly, maybe wrongly – but they think that the views expressed by Alan Walters are the views of the Prime Minister, there are . . . there is unclear direction of Government policy. Who do we believe? Do we believe the Chancellor, do we believe the . . . this 'voice' of the Prime Minister, as they take it to be? And that is very bad, you cannot conduct economic policy successfully on that basis. It is very damaging for the economy, very damaging to the Government. So I said all that to her, and I said that I'd reached the conclusion that he would have to go, he would have to go. And I said to her too, that I don't . . . I realise that it may be difficult to get rid of him, or to persuade him to go straight away, but provided he went by the end of the year, then that would be acceptable, but otherwise my position as Chancellor of the Exchequer, I regret, would be untenable.

BRIAN WALDEN:

That's a new piece of information, of course. I think most people have assumed that you demanded his *immediate* resignation, but in fact all that you were asking for is that he be removed by the end of the year?

NIGEL LAWSON:
That's right.

BRIAN WALDEN:
Did the Prime Minister say you couldn't have that?

NIGEL LAWSON:
Yes, she was unwilling to accept that.

BRIAN WALDEN:
I understand. Well, this makes it very clear . . . so that, in fact, you made it absolutely clear to her that if she was going to take that position you would have to resign?

NIGEL LAWSON:
That was precisely what I said to her. She asked me to reconsider and I said: "Yes, I will reflect on . . ." – because she said she didn't want me . . . she didn't want Alan Walters to go, but she didn't want me to resign either, and she asked me to reflect further and to recon . . . to consider what she was saying – and I said: "Of course, yes, I will reflect further – I doubt whether I will come to a different conclusion – but I will reflect further, and we'll speak again later today." And I saw her, as you know, a second time, shortly after 2 o'clock I think it was. I *had* reflected. I had come to the conclusion that, her view being what it was, I had no choice but to resign. It wasn't what I wanted to do. That wasn't, as I told the House of Commons, the outcome I sought. The outcome I sought was very clear, and that was what I'd come to her about originally . . . but that I had no alternative but to go, and I handed her, at that time, the resignation letter which you, I think, read out on your programme last week, which specifically, again, made the Alan Walters point. So – and she opened it, looked at it – so she could be in, in no doubt, in my judgment, that that was the resigning issue.

BRIAN WALDEN:
This is the account, of course, of a man who – and I think most viewers will think so – who was blindingly clear, not leaving anything open to doubt. Why do you think it is that the Prime Minister says she doesn't know why you resigned?

NIGEL LAWSON:
I've been puzzling about that. I was surprised, I watched the programme, I was surprised when she said that and I've been racking my brains, and

the only conclusion that I can come to is that she found it impossible to believe that I meant it.

BRIAN WALDEN:
Ah . . . she thought you were bluffing?

NIGEL LAWSON:
Or she thought I would back down, she thought that I wouldn't . . . I don't know what, but I think maybe she couldn't bring herself to believe that I really meant it, even though I am not somebody who plays games, and as I say we've known each other, she and I, for a considerable time. And, as I said, I had insisted on this meeting being a – all three meetings in fact, there were three, but the first one was in a sense the most important – meetings without anybody else present, no private secretary present. Most of the meetings I had with her when they were technically *tête-à-tête*, there was a private secretary present to take notes, and very often we would both speak very frankly about particular issues, and the private secretary would be there, rather anonymous figure in the corner taking a little note which wouldn't have been circulated, but a note was there, that's perfectly reasonable. But when, on this occasion, I said to her: "No, this is . . . I want to see you . . ." – and of course she said, yes, straight away – "but I want to see you privately with nobody else present" . . . she must have known because, although I'd done that from time to time in the past, it was not a normal practice, it was only when there was something very important, very serious.

BRIAN WALDEN:
Well now, this account is fascinating. Here is a man who asks for the private secretary, who normally sits in on what we might call 'bilaterals' between the Prime Minister and the Chancellor, not to be there, thus alerting the Prime Minister to the fact that something's up. He then very clearly states what it is that he objects to and makes her a proposal: that Sir Alan Walters should go by the end of the year. She declines. He then hands her a letter of resignation on that very issue. It can only be that when the Prime Minister said that she didn't know when she . . . why you had resigned, to me, that she was either lying – which I'm sure you'd want to discount – or your explanation that she thought you were bluffing. She knew what you were saying all right, but she didn't believe you. She thought you were bluffing . . . or she thought she could back you into a corner. Now, take all of that together. Doesn't it show a certain insensitivity in the Prime Minister's character, towards you at least?

NIGEL LAWSON:
Well, it saddens me and of course it disappointed me, and as I said again in the House of Commons, no one lightly gives up the great office of Chancellor of the Exchequer. I was very sorry to have to do that. But

I've done it and that is past now, and I don't think anything is to be gained by reflecting on the Prime Minister's motives or the Prime Minister's sensitivity or whatever. She was the Prime Minister, she is the Prime Minister, she was entitled to take the decision, I regret that she took the decision that she did.

BRIAN WALDEN:
That I understand. I think one thing I ought to clear up, it's the second obscurity in all this and has been the subject of a certain amount of what I would call 'black propaganda' against you. Let me ask you absolutely straight out. If the Prime Minister had said to you: "All right, Nigel, I accept your proposition, I will get rid of Alan Walters" – would you have resigned?

NIGEL LAWSON:
Yes, if it had been by the end of the year the answer is I would not have resigned.

BRIAN WALDEN:
You would not have resigned?

NIGEL LAWSON:
I would not have resigned.

BRIAN WALDEN:
So it was purely on the Walters issue that you resigned?

NIGEL LAWSON:
Absolutely. Quite clearly and categorically.

BRIAN WALDEN:
She said to me last week on this programme that she had done everything in her power to keep you. Now, how do you square that with what you've just said to me?

NIGEL LAWSON:
She did argue with me, particularly when she came back from the statement in the House of Commons at half-past-four, I think, in the afternoon. She did speak to me for a long time trying to persuade me to stay. But by that time, it was absolutely clear that she was not prepared to see Alan Walters go. And that was the only terms on which I would . . . could possibly stay. And I think any Chancellor of the Exchequer would have been in exactly the same position. Certainly, that's how I feel it. It was causing immense difficulty for the effective conduct of economic policy and this was going to be a running sore, a continuing problem for the Government as far ahead as one could see, and I felt it

was in the interests of the Government therefore that that should come to an end. As I say, I didn't want it to come to an end in the way it did, but it had to come to an end. And, if I may say one other thing too, Brian, when she had told me a year ago – I think it was a year ago, I don't want to say – that she was thinking of bringing Alan Walters back, I saw her then and I said to her that while I don't in any way dispute her right to have a personal economic adviser if she wishes to have one – may not be necessary, but I don't see . . . she has a perfect right to do that – that I thought that Alan Walters, because of the way he had been conducting himself and was likely to conduct himself, I thought this was very unwise and I urged her then not to do it. I also spoke to the Chief Whip at the time and expressed my view that there would be likely . . . not of my doing, but likely to be difficulties for the Government if he were to come back as economic adviser. So there was a little bit of history to this . . . that my concern about this goes back a long way, and the concern, alas, was vindicated by the way in which he did conduct himself during the period that he was her special economic adviser.

BRIAN WALDEN:
Sure, well all of that is clear enough that your objections to Walters were long standing; that she had known about them long before it reached any sort of crisis point; and that you would have stayed as Chancellor if she'd got rid of him. So, and I put it to you gently, the claim that she did everything in her power to keep you has to be subject to the proviso that she had it within her power to get rid of Alan Walters, and that would have kept you, wouldn't it?

NIGEL LAWSON:
That's correct.

BRIAN WALDEN:
So she didn't do everything in her power, did she?

NIGEL LAWSON:
No she didn't, but she did implore me very strongly to stay, she said she wanted me to stay, she didn't want me to go, and she was extremely kind in what she said about my job as Chancellor of the Exchequer. But no, the issue on which I had originally seen her, that, she was not disposed to change her mind about.

BRIAN WALDEN:
Well now you've known the Prime Minister a very long time, you were a close associate of her's in Opposition . . .

NIGEL LAWSON:
Yes.

BRIAN WALDEN:
. . . let alone throughout . . .

NIGEL LAWSON:
That's right.

BRIAN WALDEN:
. . . the Government. Read me the riddle of all this. Her affection for you – at least when I studied the relationship closely – never seemed to be in any very grave doubt. What is it about her these days that she cannot see . . . that she can really believe that she is doing everything in her power to keep her Chancellor, when in fact the one perfectly simple thing that she could do, which happened anyway, namely that Walters goes, she doesn't do and yet somehow she remains convinced – I'm sure you'd say honestly convinced – that she has done everything in her power. Surely this tells us something about her, doesn't it?

NIGEL LAWSON:
Well you have to re. . . form your own conclusions. I have . . .

BRIAN WALDEN:
What are yours?

NIGEL LAWSON:
I . . . the highest . . . I, no, I have the highest admiration for the Prime Minister. She's been an outstanding Prime Minister and the country has been, in my judgement, transformed during the period of her premiership over ten years. And I believe she will go on as Prime Minister for some little while to come. Historians maybe will have to ponder this, I don't think that it's helpful for me at this stage to express any further views. I'm not in the business really of expressing views on this point. What I have done is explain to you why I resigned very clearly, and what happened.

BRIAN WALDEN:
Yes, and if you don't want to pursue that matter any further I won't, because I think you have answered all the questions very clearly indeed. Let me put a different point to you. I noticed that in your speech in the House you were talking about how the Government, in fact, ought to operate. And you said that where possible – because disagreements arise, no use being foolish about this, they do between the best of friends – that they ought to be resolved privately, and whenever appropriate, collectively. Do you think what happened to you is in some ways symptomatic of a direction in which this Government is going wrong?

NIGEL LAWSON:
I think that there is something in that, because what was appearing was

a public difference. People didn't know of course how much of Alan Walters' views, as I say, truly represented the Prime Minister's views – and the Prime Minister certainly has her own views and she doesn't . . . she's no puppet, she doesn't just pick up whatever Alan Walters says. But there was an impression . . . and there had been earlier instances, which I don't particularly wish to go over, earlier instances in which it appeared that differences were being aired in public, and that is very damaging. And the Alan Walters affair, this, in a sense was an aspect of that, and that was why I said in particular that these differences – and, as you say, differences are bound to occur from time to time – these should be resolved privately. There . . . and I know for a fact there was great concern within the Party at the – and quite rightly so – about these public . . . apparent public differences being aired. Indeed the Party Conference only a short while ago, in the economic debate, one of the speakers from the floor made this very point.

BRIAN WALDEN:
Now you see, let's be quite clear as to what it is that people are objecting to about this, in the Party, I think, and you may have been hinting – indeed you've said that you *were* hinting at a real problem here. Let me define the problem. The problem is that these advisers speak to people outside 10 Downing Street, outside 11 Downing Street, outside Parliament, and they give the very distinct impression that they are speaking *on behalf* of the Prime Minister, that they are the *real voice* of the Prime Minister, and that this thing goes on unchecked to the natural fury of the ministers who feel that they are the Government. I mean that's what it's all about, isn't it?

NIGEL LAWSON:
Well, it's not just to the fury, if you like it . . . I'm not someone who is easily roused to fury . . . but it's not just the fury of the ministers, but it is also, in my opinion, to the detriment of good government.

BRIAN WALDEN:
Why does it go on then? Why can nobody put a stop to it?

NIGEL LAWSON:
I wish I'd put . . . a stop were put to it. I believe it could be and I believe it should be.

BRIAN WALDEN:
Who should do it?

NIGEL LAWSON:
I think the only person who can put a stop to it would be the Prime Minister.

BRIAN WALDEN:
Why doesn't she?

NIGEL LAWSON:
She has a great loyalty, sense of loyalty to her advisers, and loyalty is an extremely commendable characteristic. But I think that maybe it is that which stops her, maybe sometimes she isn't fully aware of everything that is being said or done. But it *is* unsatisfactory . . . it *is* unsatisfactory, and I think it would be better for the Government if that were to come to an end. I don't think it is something which is perhaps unique to this Government. I think it has tended to happen on a number of occasions in the past with different Prime Ministers. But whenever it happens, it is not good for government that it should be so.

BRIAN WALDEN:
If the Prime Minister doesn't do anything about it is there anybody else who can?

NIGEL LAWSON:
As I say, I think that this . . . it is the Prime Minister who has to consider whether there is anything that she needs to do.

BRIAN WALDEN:
Mr Lawson, you've been extremely clear and I'll – before we take the break – just put back to you what in fact, what you've told me: that you indicated in the clearest possible way what the problem was that you saw, and the problem was Sir Alan Walters; that you made the offer that he could go on till Christmas, if that was more convenient, but that after then he had to go – the Prime Minister followed this but she wouldn't give up Sir Alan Walters – consequent upon that, you resigned; that if she had have told you that she was giving up Sir Alan Walters you would have stayed; that you would not have resigned as Chancellor if she had let him go; that you have some worries, to put it mildly, about the prevalence of this kind of adviser, and that your advice to the Prime Minister would be to put an end to this particular system which can, as it did in your case, create this sort of trouble of private advisers publicly gabbing. Now that's a pretty fair summation of what we've talked about so far, isn't it?

NIGEL LAWSON:
It is.

BRIAN WALDEN:
Well now, we . . . I want to come on now to your economic policy while you *were* Chancellor but firstly we must take a break.

. . . .

BRIAN WALDEN:
Mr Lawson, we've talked about all the details of your resignation. I now want to get on to the thing that lay behind it, and that is the difference of view between yourself and Alan Walters. Now, perhaps rather than me put to you a whole series of hypotheses, perhaps you could tell viewers where it was that you and Alan Walters sharply diverged?

NIGEL LAWSON:
I mentioned in the first part that what it was concerned about was the market-sen . . . highly market-sensitive issues of interest rates, the conduct of monetary policy via interest rates, and the exchange rate. And any divergence of policy, any possibility that the government is not clear – it speaks with two voices – is extremely damaging in those particular market-sensitive areas. And it means, maybe, that policies that have to be pursued can go further than would otherwise be the case, in order to maintain credibility. The difficulty, the problem, is credibility and confidence. The art of economic management, conducting of economic policy, to a very considerable extent, is credibility and confidence: the credibility of the minister who is charged with the responsibility of carrying out the policy, and the confidence, both of business and industry, and of the financial markets, in what he is doing, and what he is saying. And the . . . it was the, if you like, the diminution of credibility and therefore the lack of confidence which was doing the great damage.

BRIAN WALDEN:
All right, now that's the political point of it, of course. Let's come to the actual economic difference. What is it *economically* about the exchange rate and about interest rates, that Alan Walters believes – possibly the Prime Minister believes – and you don't?

NIGEL LAWSON:
I think that I can best perhaps go back to what I said in my speech in the debate in the House of Commons on Tuesday, where I said that my . . . I believe that a success . . . the art of a successful economic policy is to have the greatest possible degree of market freedom within an overarching and overall financial discipline – a framework of financial discipline to bear down on inflation. And the question then is: where does the exchange rate fit in? Is it part of the market freedom, let it go where it will, wherever the markets are going to push it? Or should it be, as I believe – and I don't think Alan Walters does, I feel sure he doesn't – should it be part of the financial discipline to bear down on inflation?

BRIAN WALDEN:
In other words he wants, floating exchange rates whereas, in fact, you would like to have the greater degree of money stability that comes with managing the exchange rate. That's the real difference between you, isn't it?

NIGEL LAWSON:
That's right.

BRIAN WALDEN:
But Nigel, hadn't you used to be a free-floater?

NIGEL LAWSON:
Yes, but you know you learn, you learn with experience. And also, I'd explained very clearly in a speech I made at the IMF in Washington in 1987, in . . . why I believed that managed floating, as I described it, was better than free-floating. Partly because we had seen how in modern markets free-floating leads to extraordinary gyrations in the exchange rates, which do great damage, and which have no relation to what is really happening on the ground in the economy. And that is very disturbing to people in business and industry. And that maybe, and that maybe, at a time when inflation was very very high in many countries, maybe in those days there was no system of managing exchange rates which could have worked. Maybe then, you had to have free-floating.

BRIAN WALDEN:
Sure.

NIGEL LAWSON:
But on the whole the world is not, thank goodness, in that high inflation era now. You're better off with a greater degree of exchange rate stability. It is better for business and industry. It is better, I believe, for bringing inflation down. And, of course, some of the most successful periods of the world economy – the period of the classical Gold Standard, for example – have been periods where there have been managed exchange rates, if you like. And that is not something, therefore, that is particularly novel or particularly offensive.

BRIAN WALDEN:
Sure. All right. You've changed *your* view on that, by experience and for the reasons you've just given. Has the Prime Minister changed *hers*? Does she agree with you, or does she agree with Alan Walters?

NIGEL LAWSON:
Well you'll have to ask her that. I'm not here to answer for the Prime Minister's views. I'm here to answer for my views, but I was very glad to hear the Prime Minister, and indeed my successor John Major, both say over the past few days that they believe in a firm exchange rate.

BRIAN WALDEN:
But you see there *has* been – and I assign no blame to it, either to you or the Prime Minister or anybody else – let us say there *has* been a certain

confusion in the markets as to what the Government actually believes, between these two different propositions. What about the present Chancellor, Mr Major? Do you think he's cleared that up? Do we now know whether the Government is for managed exchange rates, or for free-floating?

NIGEL LAWSON:
As I say I am not . . . I'm here to answer for myself. I am not here to answer for . . .

BRIAN WALDEN:
Well what's your opinion then?

NIGEL LAWSON:
John Major, who is a first-class man – he worked for me as my number two at the Treasury for a little over two years – he is an excellent man – he also of course has the advantage that Alan Walters is no longer there, because Alan Walters subsequently resigned – and he has announced very clearly that he will be continuing with the policies which I was pursuing.

BRIAN WALDEN:
You said in your speech, by the way – your resignation speech – that you could well see that there was a case for free-floating, and you could well see that there was a case for using the exchange rate as part of financial discipline, but there was no case whatsoever for confusion between the two. Now, do you think that confusion has been cleared up?

NIGEL LAWSON:
I hope it has been cleared up. I'm not . . . I . . . I very much hope that it has been cleared up.

BRIAN WALDEN:
How?

NIGEL LAWSON:
I hope that it will be seen that the Government believes that the exchange rate has an essential part to play in the conduct of monetary policy generally, and in particular in imposing a financial discipline which enables us to get inflation down again. After all, you know, it was . . . it was as a result of a particularly high exchange rate then . . . but it was as a result of that, that we managed to get inflation down in the first place, when we first took office, when of course it was far higher than it is today.

BRIAN WALDEN:
But what has been said that leads you to think that the Government *has* cleared this confusion up?

NIGEL LAWSON:
I hope and believe that the . . . one of the benefits of my resignation will be the clear understanding that there has to be one voice, and one voice in economic policy, one voice particularly on matters as sensitive as interest rates and the exchange rate.

BRIAN WALDEN:
Well I wonder, you see, whether . . . I can understand that you would want the confusion cleared up. I'm not suggesting that you don't. I'm still a little bit puzzled as to why you think that your resignation has cleared it up. What is it that leads you to think that they are now going to accept the Lawson view?

NIGEL LAWSON:
Well it's not just the Lawson view, it's a pretty widespread view . . .

BRIAN WALDEN:
All right, sure.

NIGEL LAWSON:
. . . I mean we had, as you know, among the . . . first of all the Group of Five major industrial countries, and then the Group of Seven major industrial countries, agreements that we did want to secure a greater degree of stability in exchange rates during the post-1985 period, than had been the case – particularly post-1987 period – than had been the case prior to that.

BRIAN WALDEN:
Well you see, the Prime Minister was prepared to let you go, because she *wasn't* prepared to let go the man who believes in free-floating. Now surely people are going to think, at heart the Prime Minister is a free-floater, aren't they?

NIGEL LAWSON:
She said, I think very clearly on your programme, that she favoured a firm exchange rate.

BRIAN WALDEN:
No, she said she favoured a strong pound.

NIGEL LAWSON:
Or a strong pound then. A strong pound.

BRIAN WALDEN:
That isn't the same thing.

NIGEL LAWSON:
Well it's very similar, it's very similar. I think you're splitting hairs, if I may say so.

BRIAN WALDEN:
She didn't say she wanted stable exchange rates.

NIGEL LAWSON:
I think you're splitting hairs. I think you're splitting hairs. But in any event, the last thing I want to do is to cause any difficulties for my successor, to cause any difficulties for the Government. I wish the Government success. I wish the Government well. And I will continue to support it. And, as I say, I believe that it will be understood that there has to be a single voice, and I think that it will be understood that the exchange rate plays a vital part in the financial discipline that is necessary to bring down inflation.

BRIAN WALDEN:
All right. Let's move on to a point that I myself have always thought was really subsidiary to that main point – but I know you place a very great weight on it yourself – and that's this country joining the Exchange Rate Mechanism of the European Monetary System. Now, in the House you said that they should do that really as soon as possible. In some ways that's a movement from what you said at Madrid. Do you think they are going to join the Exchange Rate Mechanism as soon as possible?

NIGEL LAWSON:
No, I don't think that is any sense, incidentally, a movement from what is known as the Madrid formula. The Madrid formula and the . . . to put it in context, there were discussions obviously between the Prime Minister and Geoffrey Howe, who was then Foreign Secretary, and I, who was then Chancellor, before Madrid, on our approach to the Delors . . . so-called Delors plan for European monetary union – the various stages. And we all agreed we could accept Stage One, not Stages Two and Three . . . and Stage One, which involved a whole lot of things including British full membership of the EMS, including the Exchange Rate Mechanism, and on equal terms with the other currencies, that is to say the same margins. And the formula then . . . I wasn't at Madrid, Madrid was . . . Madrid European Council was attended by the Prime Minister and Geoffrey Howe – finance ministers are below the salt . . . beneath the salt, they don't get invited to these grand things like European Councils, even though financial matters are being discussed, but that's by the by – and er . . . but the Madrid formula was that we reaffirmed that it was . . . it came out as recently as this week, or a few days ago, in a paper which was put out by the Treasury, by . . . on behalf of the Government, called *An Evolutionary Path to Monetary*

Union, saying clearly we reaffirmed – and this is the Madrid formula – we reaffirmed our . . . that we would join the EMS fully, the Exchange Rate Mechanism of the EMS, once inflation was lower and the exchange controls . . . free . . .

BRIAN WALDEN:
But you'd join straight away wouldn't you, without worrying about those conditions?

NIGEL LAWSON:
. . . no . . . and the abolition of exchange controls and certain other . . . progress on certain other aspects of the so-called single market. Now, I accepted those conditions and I still do. Though on the exchange control point, and I'm sorry to take so long . . .

BRIAN WALDEN:
It's all right.

NIGEL LAWSON:
But on the exchange control point – which, incidentally, I was the first to put this forward publicly at . . . when I appeared before the Treasury select committee, before Madrid – it is reasonable to wait until the first of July next year when both France and Italy are due to abolish their exchange controls, because there are some people who say it is only these exchange controls that are propping this ramshackle edifice up, once those are gone the whole thing will collapse. And I believe that is wrong, and incidentally the Governor of the Bank of England, when he gave evidence, also said in his judgement that is not so. But the proof of the pudding is in the eating, so let's wait and see. Let these exchange controls be removed and then see whether it is still there for us to join. So it's reasonable to wait till then. But, you know, these Madrid conditions, or Madrid terms, which were, in an effect, a kind of compromise, these can be interpreted in different ways, how soon . . .

BRIAN WALDEN:
A fudge in other words.

NIGEL LAWSON:
. . . not a fudge. It is a sensible way for Government to conduct itself – not to get boxed into an over-rigid position. But it enables the Government to decide when inflation is low enough, when there's been sufficient progress on these other matters . . . and my view, which I expressed in the House of Commons, that we should seek a positive approach to this, and seek to do it early rather than at the last possible moment, that was what I was saying.

BRIAN WALDEN:
But you see because it *is* a fudge the Prime Minister can interpret it quite differently, can't she, and make sure that you go in at the last possible moment, or not go in at all?

NIGEL LAWSON:
Well we have committed ourselves that we are going in, and there is . . . I am sure . . .

BRIAN WALDEN:
But she can still do that, can't she?

NIGEL LAWSON:
. . . well yes I . . . although there was a report – I don't know, it was after I'd left the government – but there was a report I was interested to read a few days ago, saying that the Prime Minister accepted that the question of when to join the ERM was a matter for collective decision, and not a matter for her alone. But there is also a . . . a political angle.

BRIAN WALDEN:
You think, in other words, you think the Cabinet might overrule her on this?

NIGEL LAWSON:
That . . . I think a collective matter and not a matter for her alone. That was the report which I read . . . that was the report which I read . . .

BRIAN WALDEN:
You *do* think that they are going to overrule her don't you?

NIGEL LAWSON:
. . . no, that was the report which I read.

BRIAN WALDEN:
All right.

NIGEL LAWSON:
But clearly . . . no she will . . . she will have to form her own view, obviously, but in the context, I would hope, of a collective decision on this matter. I believe that is what she said, and I think that is right. But anyhow, there is also a political dimension, too. I am very concerned, just as she is, that we have the right kind of Europe: a Europe of nation states, not a federal Europe; a Europe which is a free market Europe, not a bureaucratic *dirigiste* form of Europe. And the question is: how can we best exert Britain's influence? Many people may say we shouldn't be in the European Community at all. Maybe – but that is not the view of the

Government, that is not the policy of the Government. We *are* within the European Community, and therefore the important question is: how can we best exercise Britain's influence in that community in order to get the sort of Europe that we believe in, and indeed in order to promote the interests of this country most effectively? That is what I want to see. And we can, I believe exer . . . we will not be able to exert that influence, nearly as effectively as we should, so long as we remain outside, fully not . . . outside, really, the EMS.

BRIAN WALDEN:
A last question on ERM and of the EMS. Should members of the Cabinet insist that this decision be collective?

NIGEL LAWSON:
It's a matter for the Prime Minister to decide and it's a matter for the Cabinet to decide. I'm not a member of the Cabinet any more, and it is for my successors.

BRIAN WALDEN:
How would you advise . . .

NIGEL LAWSON:
I would hope that . . . I would hope that there will be a collective discussion of this at a reasonably early date, it doesn't have to be this week, or next week.

BRIAN WALDEN:
All right, well now I think we've gone through every conceivable issue that we could have done, I must say as far as clarity goes, to my great satisfaction, but of course I can't let you off the programme, as we come to the end, without remembering that you *were* Chancellor, and putting that point to you. A lot of people say, you see: "Well it's all very well for Lawson to go on about this that and the other. No wonder Mrs Thatcher wanted Sir Alan Walters. Look at the mess he'd managed to get her into. Naturally she'd want a second opinion after all of that. Look what he did: he slackened off the monetary discipline, in his Mansion House speech of '85, and it went altogether in '86; he stopped targetting money, let all that loose on the economy; then he shadowed the Deutschmark, without Cabinet permission, without fully discussing it with the Prime Minister; then there were his tax cuts, all of which fed demand. This man has an appalling record. He used to have a good record, he used to believe in keeping inflation down. Now he doesn't. He believed in growth. He gambled and he lost, and he created an appalling mess and that's why I've got a disastrous mortgage, because look where interest rates had to go to – 15 per cent – in order to cover for all of this." Now, what is the general, blanket Lawson defence to that – as you know – frequent charge?

NIGEL LAWSON:
Well the blanket defence is that I don't accept, basically, any of it. Certainly inflation . . .

BRIAN WALDEN:
No mistakes at all?

NIGEL LAWSON:
No, I'm saying . . . not talking about no mistakes . . . though of course people make mistakes, and I've made my share of mistakes, but I'm talking about the particular points that you raised. It is certainly not true that I am unconcerned about inflation. I am deeply concerned about getting inflation down, and indeed the lowest we've had inflation during the whole of the period of this Government – and I say this not to in any way decry Geoffrey Howe. Geoffrey Howe as Chancellor did a tremendous job, and all I did was to build on the foundations which he laid. And of course the Prime Minister too, was the third minister, if you like, who's had a . . . a major role in the conduct of economic policy over this period. And I believe it has been a period of success. In fact I'm convinced of that, and so is the Prime Minister, she said so on your programme only last Sunday, and the British economy . . .

BRIAN WALDEN:
At length.

NIGEL LAWSON:
. . . at considerable length, and I agree with everything she said, and the British economy *has* been transformed. And what we have now is . . . certainly is a temporary upsurge of inflation, which we have to get on top of. And that is why I took the very tough decisions. I have not, as it were, run away because I'm not prepared to take tough decisions. I took the tough decisions to put interest rates up as high as was necessary in order to get on top of inflation and I believe that has been done, and I believe that inflation has already peaked. I also was able to ensure that we had a tight fiscal position, that is to say a budget surplus, not a deficit, as there's been in previous times. As for abandoning targetting money, I didn't do that at all. Experience showed that so-called broad money – the sterling M3, as it was then – so-called broad money was a very very poor guide to conditions in the economy. Narrow money, M-nought, was a very much better guide and therefore I switched from targetting the broad money to targetting the narrow money, and we retain narrow money targets to this day . . .

BRIAN WALDEN:
All right.

NIGEL LAWSON:
And as for the tax cuts, the tax cuts were vitally necessary in order to create a more dynamic economy and we've already seen the benefits of that, we've already seen the much improved performance of British business and industry. Now, of course all sorts of things went . . . not quite as I expected, but that's not surprising in a free economy.

BRIAN WALDEN:
All right, let me put . . . we're coming towards the end, let me put this to you, you see. You *did* reduce inflation quite substantially, I think it was down to 3.4 at its lowest.

NIGEL LAWSON:
No, the low . . . it was down to two-and-a-half . . . I had 2.4 per cent at one point.

BRIAN WALDEN:
All right, well now look. It's not the worst sin in the world. Why not admit it? Having conquered inflation, being a lively fellow and by nature something of a gambler, you thought you could get both, didn't you? Low inflation, *and* high growth. And you went for the high growth and it didn't quite work, did it?

NIGEL LAWSON:
How did I go for the high growth? Of course I didn't go for the high growth. What I went for throughout was a tight monetary policy and a tight fiscal policy . . .

BRIAN WALDEN:
But you boosted demand.

NIGEL LAWSON:
. . . incidentally everybody says . . . no I didn't, I didn't boost demand at all. So, far from boosting demand by pouring money into the economy, the budget surplus increased, we had the biggest budget surplus we've ever had . . .

BRIAN WALDEN:
But the money got there somehow, Nigel, didn't it?

NIGEL LAWSON:
Yes, yes it did, it did, because we had a huge . . . as a result of financial freedom and as a result of the great upsurge of confidence there was in the country, we got people borrowing on an enormous and unprecedented scale. Just think of two figures alongside each other: the tax cuts in the 1988 budget – which I think are highly desirable and will have continuing

beneficial effects – they amounted to four billion; the increase in personal borrowing amounted to forty billion. It was this huge upsurge of borrowing, far greater than anything I expected . . .

BRIAN WALDEN:
Mr Lawson, I must stop you. Thank you very much indeed.

NIGEL LAWSON:
Thank you.

LABOUR'S CRISIS OF CREDIBILITY

OF ALL THE POLITICAL DEVELOPMENTS to affect Britain in 1989, it was the transformation of the Labour Party which seemed the most important. As long as Labour looked unelectable, the Conservatives could afford to have a leader with an unpopular style of government, and the parties of the centre could credibly bid for a piece of the political action. But the appearance of Labour's Policy Review in May made it look as though both the Tories and the centre parties might soon be facing a much more difficult time. With the publication of this document, long-standing commitments to policies like nationalisation and unilateral nuclear disarmament, which the voters seemed determined to reject, were unceremoniously dumped. At the Labour Party Conference in October, Neil Kinnock seemed to have no difficulty in getting his party to accept this new policy stance. Labour seemed well placed to recover its traditional role as the only credible alternative to the Conservatives and, given the Government's growing troubles, perhaps to sweep to power at the next election.

Yet there were doubts. It was now clear what the Labour Party was not. But what had it become? Many considered the Policy Review did not provide a clear and convincing new philosophy to replace the one on which the old policies had been based. And as the autumn progressed, Labour's front bench spokesmen did not convince everybody that their remarks on the questions of the hour reflected a coherent body of convincing policies. Indeed, some accused Labour of opportunistically exploiting the Conservatives' difficulties by opposing whatever they were doing without offering a credible alternative.

It was on the economic front that doubts like these were most acute. In the past, persuading voters that Labour could be trusted with the nation's finances had always been one of the party's greatest problems. In the Policy Review, much stress was laid on new methods of reconstructing Britain's shrunken industrial base, but these seemed to have much in common with the failed techniques of previous Labour governments. We decided that *The Walden Interview* should question Labour's then up-and-coming Trade and Industry Spokesman, Bryan Gould, about these policies. But by the time he was to appear, much more pressing economic issues had presented themselves.

Rising inflation, record balance of payments deficits and soaring interest rates were stoking fears of economic crisis which came to a head on the day Mr Gould was due to appear, 15 October. A sudden fall in Wall Street prices the previous Friday had raised the spectre of a new "Black Monday" on the London stock market the following day. At that moment, it seemed unlikely that anybody would want to hear about Labour's long-term plans for the industrial base, but it seemed quite possible that some people might be wondering whether the party would be any better than the Conservatives at short-term economic management. The then Chancellor, Nigel Lawson, was insisting that priority must be given to the fight against inflation and that in the short term high interest rates were the only effective weapon against it. In the longer term he was thought to be looking towards membership of the exchange rate mechanism of the European Monetary System, but Mrs Thatcher was believed to be opposing him on this. Labour was thought to have its own split on the EMS, to be unsure how high a priority it put on the fight against inflation and to have no idea how its supposed alternative to high interest rates, credit control, could actually be made to work.

Strictly speaking, these were matters for the Shadow Chancellor, John Smith, but he was away in Europe and we decided that his front bench colleague could be expected to explain the party's policies on his behalf. Mr Gould seemed to think so too, and all might have been well if the party's policies had in fact been properly formulated. When we came to credit controls, Walden pointed out that since most personal credit was for house purchase, effective credit control must mean curbs on mortgages. Mr Gould did not demur. So who would be denied mortages? Not first-time buyers, said Mr Gould: that left people who were "trading up", including, in Walden's lethal phrase, "growing families".

At last Labour had a policy on credit control which made good sense. It was also about to kiss goodbye to lots of votes from those who had, or thought they might have, growing families, to the glee of the morrow's right-wing press. Mr Smith moved quickly to deny that mortgage controls formed any part of Labour's policy, which left the party's Deputy Leader, Roy Hattersley, with something to explain when he turned up on *The Walden Interview* the following Sunday. Nor was this all he had to explain.

We had called in Mr Hattersley, the thinker of the Front Bench team, to deal not just with specific policy questions but also with that more fundamental doubt. Had Labour thrown out its soul with those unpopular left-wing policies? What exactly did it stand for nowadays? Leader writers had come to re-interpret this question as the problem of the 'big idea'. The new-look Labour Party, it was suggested, needed to offer voters a grand philosophical concept. We decided to ask Mr Hattersley if it would.

The question was an awkward one because the party had previously had a 'big idea' which had never been explicitly disavowed. This notion was of course socialism, which met all the leader writers' requirements of a big idea, but was something which Labour's leaders now seemed most anxious not to mention lest it should frighten voters. Would Mr Hattersley come up with one of the new big ideas which the leader writers were offering? Or would he feel obliged to go for a sanitised version of socialism, and in so doing undo much of the work of Labour's image builders?

15TH OCTOBER, 1989

BRIAN WALDEN INTERVIEWS BRYAN GOULD

BRIAN WALDEN:
A stock market crash could well occur tomorrow. If it does and interest rates stay at 15 per cent, a full-scale recession could take place. What should the Government do, and could Labour manage things any better? Bryan Gould, one of the Labour Party's main front bench spokesmen on economic affairs, is with me today.

Mr Gould, last week Mr Lawson, the Chancellor of the Exchequer, committed himself to a very, very firm anti-inflationary strategy, implying that, even though interest rates were high, they may even have to go higher if necessary in order to squeeze inflation out of the system. On Friday, Wall Street fell precipitously and there are those who think that when the markets open tomorrow we may be in for a Stock Exchange crash as bad if not worse as that of October 1987. Now, if Mr Lawson persists with his present policy, what will be the consequences of that?

BRYAN GOULD:
Well, I think quite clearly we are an economy now teetering on the brink of recession. It's not just that we have the massive trade deficit, the very high interest rates, the unduly high inflation rate, at least in comparative terms, but we have a good deal of survey evidence from the CBI, a great deal of evidence that British industry is finding the going very tough indeed. And indeed one of the reasons why the Chancellor's strategy is not working is that his chosen instrument of high interest rates may be effective, no-one disputes this, in damping down demand eventually, but in the course of doing so it's doing great damage to British industry, and that I think is what is likely to tip us over the brink. Now, if you add to that not only the damage to the property market, the damage to retail sales, all of that, the damage to Britain's competitiveness in manufacturing markets and so on . . . if you add to that the further recessionary impetus that could come from a stock market fall then I suspect, as many other people do, that that may be enough to push us over that brink and that the

Chancellor's problems will then be – the nightmare of every Chancellor no doubt – that he's facing and grappling with the problems of recession on the one hand and inflation on the other, but he cannot, as it were, choose a course which deals with them both at the same time. And that's Mr Chan . . . Mr Lawson's problem and that's why all the cheers he received in Blackpool last week cannot, I think, really obscure the fact that he has made very substantial mistakes in economic policy and has left himself in a position where it's not easy to see where he now goes.

BRIAN WALDEN:
That's clear and of course there are aspects of that I want to probe. But before I do . . . when they had this problem in October '87 he was worried of course that we would topple into a recession and he then cut interest rates. What do you think the Government will do this time?

BRYAN GOULD:
I don't know what they're going to do because I think the situation is different from that which obtained in 1987. You're quite right, in 1987 he cut interest rates and that, I think, was arguably, let's be charitable – I'm not always as uncharitable to my political opponents as some people would like me to be but let's be charitable – I think arguably at the time that was a rational response to that situation. What went wrong, of course, was that he then compounded what we now see to have been an error by bringing in tax cuts, which we warned him against, and by presiding over a great explosion of private credit, which I think has done the real damage. Nevertheless, it could be argued that at that time, although we had an incipient trade deficit rearing its ugly head, that nevertheless the fundamentals of the economy could have been argued to have been okay. I don't myself accept that that was the case but at least the truth was being obscured for the time being by North Sea oil and a consumer boom and so on. Today however it's very plain, frighteningly plain that the fundamentals are out of kilter; that he doesn't have that same room for manoeuvre; that if he cuts interest rates now he has to do the almost impossible feat of standing on his head, reversing in mid-progress the very direction that he told us just last week was his only and central priority. So I cannot myself see that having put the economy through such pain in the interests of that central and overriding objective of getting on top of inflation, and proclaiming time and again over 15 months – twelve successive interest rate increases – that this is the only instrument which will work, he cannot now in my view reverse all of that, slam the brakes off . . . on, and then head off in exactly the opposite direction.

BRIAN WALDEN:
So plainly, you don't think he will cut interest rates. I mean, leave aside whether he should, you don't think he will?

BRYAN GOULD:
I would be astonished if he were to do that.

BRYAN WALDEN:
All right, now let's hear a word or two on something else that the Labour Party often mentions and indeed others, too. You see, the recession *didn't* happen after October '87, and that, some people say, has led to profound disagreements between the Chancellor and the Prime Minister. He chose to go for growth and avoid a recession. She blames him for having done that, so some people say. Of course, it may be that she doesn't, but the word is about that she does and that she thinks he brought inflation into the system. Now, do you think a similar disagreement could break out this time?

BRYAN GOULD:
I think it's the same disagreement. I don't think it's gone away. I think it is something that explains a good deal of the course of our economic policy and obviously of the relations between the Prime Minister and the Chancellor over that whole period . . . and I'm sorry to say on this occasion I'm not going to be so charitable to the Chancellor because I think what is really at stake here is the Chancellor's concern to protect his own reputation. I think in his more honest moments he would concede, indeed I think he has conceded, that mistakes were made at about the time you're directing our attention to. I think the Prime Minister believes that very strongly. She's said as much. The question is what do you do about that mistake? The Prime Minister's instincts – and here although I disagree with her analysis, I think she was right – her instincts were to say, "Yes, the mistake has been made, we have to pay the price. There's no way we can avoid paying the price in terms of inflation or whatever it may be. Let's get it out of the way as soon as possible. Let's pay the price, let's say if necessary mea culpa, but let's now reassure the money markets that henceforth monetarist discipline is re-established." The Chancellor's interest however is a rather different one. He's unwilling, I think, to concede that that mistake was made, at least in any great measure. He doesn't want to be seen as the Chancellor who forces the economy to pay an unpleasant price, and so his strategy is to fiddle his way through, to try and achieve that soft landing which, I think, has the effect only of prolonging the difficulties. And the difficulties are now prolonged to such a degree, with no sign that they're about to be resolved, that I think the Chancellor is in great danger of getting his election timing wrong.

BRIAN WALDEN:
Doesn't that all imply that one or the other of them ought to go? Now, plainly it's not going to be her . . . so that, in effect, you are saying that it would positively assist Britain's financial difficulties if the Prime Minister sacked the Chancellor and replaced him with someone which she did have confidence in?

BRYAN GOULD:
I think . . . it's not for me to say what's in the Prime Minister's mind, but I'm sure that that thought is not far from her thinking . . . the only qualification I would make is that I think the time for taking that action is . . .

BRIAN WALDEN:
. . . has gone . . .

BRYAN GOULD:
. . . the optimum time has gone. I was one of those few people in the Spring of this year who believed that the Chancellor might actually go, for the very reason I've just described. I think having bitten the bullet as it were, having decided to live with the Chancellor, to give his interest rate policy a whirl for yet another six months or so, I think it's very difficult for the Prime Minister now to say, "Hang on, we were all wrong back in March. I should have sacked him then." I think she's now committed to a degree that she wasn't then, and I think the damage that's been done really is now damage for which she must share part of the responsibility as well. So it's not so easy for her to walk away from the wreckage, a wreckage that she would certainly see as including Mr . . . Chancellor Lawson.

BRIAN WALDEN:
Well, your view will be very well received down at Number 11, that he's more or less, he's not light on this nest, he's more or less stuck there for the moment. Obviously, I've asked you about these things, not to get an impartial view – you wouldn't claim to be impartial – but to get an insight on this very nervous, tense weekend of how Labour's thinking. Let me move quite directly now to the Labour Party itself and your view of a Stock Exchange crash. Let's suppose you came in tomorrow morning and let's suppose there was a stock market crash of very considerable dimensions. What I really want to get at first is what would be the worry in your mind and the mind of Labour's Chancellor and indeed Labour's Prime Minister and first of all of the Treasury . . . which way would the main burden of the worry be falling? Would you be worried about inflation or would you be worried principally about recession?

BRYAN GOULD:
I think the view I would take – and I think this is certainly the view that my colleagues take – is that in the end it really doesn't make sense to believe that we have a range of different problems. I think the problem is one central problem. It manifests itself in different ways. It manifests itself in our constant propensity to inflate faster than other countries, in our constant propensity to import more than other countries, and in our

constant propensity therefore to slide into recession as soon as we have to slam the brakes on in order to deal with those other problems. What I think we have to be clear about, and if I had one simple point that I would want to try to get across in conversation with you, it is that there is no . . . there is nothing a Labour Government or any other government could do tomorrow or the day after. There is no magic button which is going to revolutionise our prospects overnight. We are paying a price, I believe, for constantly believing that there are short-term solutions to our problems when indeed those problems are deep seated and long term. And the longer we ignore the need to grapple with them on that long-term basis then the worse they become, and the more we wriggle on the hook as we opt and jump, as it were, from one short-term solution to another.

BRIAN WALDEN:
All right, suppose I accept that – and if there's time I will talk to you about some of the long-term things later. In this wicked world as you well know Bryan, there will be some people watching who will say, ah hang on, I smell a fudge. From what Mr Gould said earlier I got the impression that he was much more worried about a recession. Now when asked straight out: "If you were in power would you be more worried about that or more worried about inflation?" – he hedges a bit.' What would be your answer to that?

BRYAN GOULD:
Well, I think the answer would be that since you were kind enough to . . . and I hope you will persist with this theme – you give me the chance then to elaborate what was, necessarily I think, an introductory remark on the nature of the problem . . .

BRIAN WALDEN:
Sure.

BRYAN GOULD:
. . . but what I think, what I would then say to follow up that introductory point, is that I think we have to be much more specific then, having accepted that there is this general long-term problem on which we have to work over the long term, I think in terms of dealing with it in the short term, and you're absolutely right to say that it is necessary to make a short-term response . . .

BRIAN WALDEN:
That's right.

BRYAN GOULD:
. . . I think we have to distinguish between measures that are designed to deal with inflation on the one hand and with the prospect of recession

on the other. And I don't necessarily think that we're committed to a course of policy – whatever it might be – which necessarily forces us to choose between those two objectives. Let me tell you what I mean. If our problem is fundamentally, or has been for some time, inflation, looked at as a short-term phenomenon – that is demand has got out of hand – that I think is primarily because the Chancellor allowed a credit explosion to take place: huge volumes of credit created by the banking sector and in particular by the building societies. That's where this immense purchasing power which sucked in imports and has pushed up inflation – that's where it came from. I think if we are worried about inflation we should be dealing with that problem . . .

BRIAN WALDEN:
Ah.

BRYAN GOULD:
. . . not through interest rates across the board, because interest rates while certainly dealing with that problem, actually make the prospects of recession more bleak and bring them closer. So that we should be dealing as I argue with inflation by rather more specific measures, to try and damp down that element of demand, but doing so in such a way that we're not handicapping ourselves in trying to build the supply side strength of British industry which is in the end the only way we're going to grapple with recession.

BRIAN WALDEN:
All right, now credit controls certainly, I want to have a word with you about those. But what about interest rates? Do you think they ought to stay as they are or come down?

BRYAN GOULD:
Well again your notional viewer, your hypothetical viewer will say, oh we can see he's wriggling, he's hedging. But I think I'm not . . .

BRIAN WALDEN:
Which you're not of course . . . you're not, you're going to give me a straight answer. I can see that coming . . .

BRYAN GOULD:
What I think I'm entitled to say, again by way of preliminary – and I will try to answer your question in a moment – but by way of preliminary comment, I think we are entitled to use the Irishman's answer: we wouldn't have started from here. We've been warning, after all, for three years . . .

BRIAN WALDEN:
But you would if you came in tomorrow morning.

BRYAN GOULD:
Yes . . . oh sure sure. Sure, but nevertheless let me just make this preliminary point because very often the economic debate is presented in terms of immense competence on behalf of the Tory Government and a Labour Party which really doesn't know what it's talking about. On this occasion, and on the central question, it is the Labour Party over the course of three years which has correctly analysed and forecast our economic difficulties. It's the Chancellor – and if you give me a chance I'll detail this in a moment or two – it's the Chancellor who has been all over the shop, got his forecast wrong, pushed up the pound, held it down, done all sorts of things. Now having said all that, having said that we would not therefore have relied upon successive rises in the interest rate and therefore we wouldn't have created this inherently unstable structure, teetering on the basis of interest rates and an exchange rate which probably can't be sustained . . .

BRIAN WALDEN:
But now you've got it . . .

BRYAN GOULD:
. . . having said all that, now that we come to power as it were tomorrow, and I wish it were true, then I think we would want to say that there is no future for British industry, there is no future for escaping recession if we persist in holding interest rates as high as they are at present . . .

BRIAN WALDEN:
So you'd cut them?

BRYAN GOULD:
We would begin the process of bringing them down, relying on other instruments to deal with the immediate short term problem of excessive demand, but also trying to create the conditions in which British industry, which is after all the other important part of the equation, in which British industry can begin to improve their competitiveness, both in the long term through investment, and in the short term by being able to compete in the markets for which they have to compete both at home and abroad.

BRIAN WALDEN:
Okay you'd cut interest rates, by how much?

BRYAN GOULD:
Well, that I think is not a question that you can expect me to answer. Since we would not have got ourselves to 15 per cent in the first place, we would not I think want to be clear – and no Chancellor or no Secretary of

State for Trade and Industry for that matter would say in advance that we intended to reach a certain level of interest rates – what we would say, however, is that we saw the future trend of interest rates as being downwards. Now how far we would . . .

BRIAN WALDEN:
Substantially downwards?

BRYAN GOULD:
Well, I think we would certainly – since we've argued against each successive rise in interest rates . . .

BRIAN WALDEN:
That's right.

BRYAN GOULD:
. . . I'm not necessarily saying that we would in one leap want to go back to where the Chancellor had them when they were seven-and-a-half per cent – but we would certainly see – just as the Chancellor was inclined to say fifteen . . . eighteen months ago . . . fifteen months ago that he would move interest rates up as necessary – I think we would say that we would want to see interest rates moving down commensurate with our other objectives. Of course if we felt . . .

BRIAN WALDEN:
At about the same pace that he put them up?

BRYAN GOULD:
Well, that very much depends on the course of the real economy. Again – if I can make this point which I think is a point of real and substantial difference between the approach we would take to the economy, and that which the Chancellor has followed – we would want to look very closely at real economy indicators, not just at things like money supply or whatever measure of the money supply the Chancellor currently favours – M-nought I believe – or at things like exchange rates just looked at in a vacuum. We would want to see whether there were signs that British industry's competitiveness was indeed improving, whether the trade deficit was getting smaller, that's what we would be aiming at. But we would not of course, move from the centre of our economic objectives the need to reduce inflation – it's far too high at present. For all those who say that the Tories are at least sound on inflation, let's be quite clear it's the present government which took risks with inflation, has been all over the shop as I say, and which has produced an inflation rate which is now the highest in the advanced industrial world.

BRIAN WALDEN:
All right, now we've had your views clearly and at adequate length – and necessary length – on all of these things. Can I . . . I'm a man of my word and I want to come back to credit controls . . . can I for a moment put this idea of cutting interest rates on the back-burner? Of course I want to come back to that, but let's have a go at credit controls for the moment. I rather took it from the way you put it to me, that . . . of course you don't want to put credit controls on capital borrowing. I mean, we can agree that, can't we?

BRYAN GOULD:
Yes.

BRIAN WALDEN:
So it's consumer borrowing that you want to put it on. Now you don't just want to put it on the fifteen per cent that isn't mortgages, do you? You want to put it on mortgages as well?

BRYAN GOULD:
Well let me, since we're on the subject of credit controls which I very much welcome, let me first say that the notion that you can control credit exclusively through price dates from Ted Heath – competition and credit control in the early 70s. It's a view which has dominated British economic policy-making over the period since then, with one or two exceptions . . . brief exceptions. It's not a view which is shared elsewhere. If you look to rather more successful economies, if you look to Germany, West Germany for example you will find there the Bundesbank exercising a powerful control over lending by the banking sector. They use . . .

BRIAN WALDEN:
But not by credit controls?

BRYAN GOULD:
Well, you see I think there is some misunderstanding of what is meant by credit control.

BRIAN WALDEN:
Now let me tell you what the Bundesbank does . . .

BRYAN GOULD:
Absolutely.

BRIAN WALDEN:
. . . and you tell me how it can be called a credit control. What the Bundesbank does is to make the clearing banks in Germany place

reserves with it. It varies the nature of those reserves when it wants to . . .

BRYAN GOULD:
That's right.

BRIAN WALDEN:
. . . But once it's done that, those independent banks then use interest rates just like our banks do, don't they?

BRYAN GOULD:
Oh sure, oh sure.

BRIAN WALDEN:
But that's not a credit control?

BRYAN GOULD:
Oh well it is, because . . . yes yes. These are measures which we used to call things like special deposits or the corset. These were, if you like, actual physical controls. Now what I'm saying, is that our first port of call, if you like, in facing up to the problem of the huge explosion, huge explosion, unprecedented explosion, in bank lending, building society lending for private consumption, our first port of call ought to be to look to the successful experience of other countries and what more successful experience than that of West Germany, that's the first point.

BRIAN WALDEN:
But, but well let's come back to that . . .

BRYAN GOULD:
Right, OK.

BRIAN WALDEN:
Let's come back to that, because I'm not suggesting for a second you intend to and I'm not suggesting there's any viewer who is like this, but it is just possible that an innocent viewer somewhere may be slightly deceived by that little bit. If you are going to say that what the Bundesbank does is what the Labour Party has meant by credit restriction, let me point out of course that the effect of pulling the deposits in and then saying to the clearing banks, "All right, use price from now on", means that your sort of credit restriction would put interest rates up, not down, wouldn't it?

BRYAN GOULD:
Not necessarily, because if . . . when we get on to the point of industrial strategy, you would then find, I think, that we have some notion of what priority ought to be given to varying forms of lending . . .

BRIAN WALDEN:
But that's very long term . . .

BRYAN GOULD:
Well no, no, no, no . . .

BRYAN GOULD:
. . . come on, short term it would put it up, wouldn't it?

BRYAN GOULD:
Well it depends, it depends entirely on the demand that there would then be for credit. Now the demand for credit in Britain at present is very largely fuelled – and here we get on to the second part of the argument to which you wanted to direct me in the first place . . .

BRIAN WALDEN:
Sure.

BRYAN GOULD:
. . . is very or has been very largely fuelled by the asset inflation created by the huge preponderance of mortgage lending as an element in our personal credit . . .

BRIAN WALDEN:
That's right.

BRYAN GOULD:
. . . and the degree to which that has had two effects, I think. One it is split over into other forms of spending; the controls, if you like – in other words the purposes for which mortgage lending is made – have not been rigorously enough controlled. So great . . . everybody knows this. I've done it myself. Many of your viewers will know what I mean when on switching houses they have deliberately gone for a larger mortgage than they need in order to produce a bit of extra spending.

BRIAN WALDEN:
Sure.

BRYAN GOULD:
So that's the first thing. The second thing is, that because that form of credit has been totally, almost entirely unrestrained and has burgeoned to such a degree, the effect of that has been to create a degree of asset inflation – mainly house prices, first in the South East then in the rest of the country – which has induced as it were a psychological mood on the part of many people, that without doing anything they can sit at home and watch their wealth grow day by day, and that has induced a

willingness then to go out to take on other forms of borrowing, other forms of credit.

BRIAN WALDEN:
Sure.

BRYAN GOULD:
And that I think is where the problem has arisen.

BRIAN WALDEN:
So you're going to restrict mortgages?

BRYAN GOULD:
Well, I think what we have to be clear about – and the Chancellor is clear about this as well – I noticed in his speech he pointed out that eighty-five per cent of personal borrowing takes the form of mortgage advances.

BRIAN WALDEN:
That's right.

BRYAN GOULD:
So we're not talking about the familiar aspects of credit control, the hire purchase restrictions, limiting credit cards and so on – these are not big elements. But what we're saying, is that if there is a problem in terms of managing the degree of credit growth in this economy it has to be at the margin when new mortgages are being granted. We're not talking about penalising existing mortgages . . .

BRIAN WALDEN:
But now . . . well now hang on you see, Mr Gould. This if I may say so is very interesting stuff indeed . . .

BRYAN GOULD:
I'd hoped you'd find it so.

BRIAN WALDEN:
. . . because you know as well as I do that a lot of people have assumed that when the Labour Party talked about credit controls, what it had in mind was that fifteen per cent that *did* have to do with plastic cards and . . .

BRYAN GOULD:
Exactly.

BRIAN WALDEN:
. . . hire purchase . . .

BRYAN GOULD:
Yes.

BRIAN WALDEN:
. . . and all that. They have thought that. Now you're saying something very interesting indeed. You're saying no it doesn't. We're going to attack the problem where the problem really is . . .

BRYAN GOULD:
That's right.

BRIAN WALDEN:
. . . which is the eighty-five per cent of borrowing for mortgages.

BRYAN GOULD:
That's right.

BRIAN WALDEN:
Right, no new mortgages, eh?

BRYAN GOULD:
No we're not saying no new mortgages. But what we're saying is . . .

BRIAN WALDEN:
Very strict conditions for new mortgages.

BRYAN GOULD:
Well strict*er* conditions.

BRIAN WALDEN:
Ah!

BRYAN GOULD:
I mean there are conditions: twenty-five years is generally thought to be the permissible term for a mortgage . . . three times the gross salary might well be regarded by many building societies as about the maximum that they would lend. These are controls, limits if you like, which can be adjusted and which we believe ought to be adjusted, if that form of lending and borrowing is growing too fast.

BRIAN WALDEN:
I understand. But obviously I want details, further details on this if I can get them because it is important. I mean this is . . . this has come out of left field . . . this is . . .

BRYAN GOULD:
No, no, no let me make this clear. I attach enormous importance of course to appearing on your programme . . . and I hope . . .

BRIAN WALDEN:
But you've said it before.

BRYAN GOULD:
That's right . . .

BRIAN WALDEN:
That's what you're going to tell me . . .

BRYAN GOULD:
Absolutely right.

BRIAN WALDEN:
They always tell me this.

BRYAN GOULD:
I have done my damnedest let me assure you to get this point across, but there is a . . . you're quite right there is a problem in using the term credit controls.

BRIAN WALDEN:
That's right . . .

BRYAN GOULD:
Because people's memories immediately go back to hire purchase restrictions and so on.

BRIAN WALDEN:
That's right, that's right. We . . . what we are getting here in fact – you may at some stage have said it before – we're getting it here in a particularly dramatic form, at a particularly dramatic moment. Let me put to you something about it that people often argue about. They say: "But of course if you try and clamp down on new mortgages," and you've suggested one way of doing it, "it will inevitably hit young couples . . ."

BRYAN GOULD:
Yes.

BRIAN WALDEN:
". . . they will be the people who'll suffer." Now you would agree that that is so, wouldn't you?

BRYAN GOULD:
Yes, I think that is a real worry and that is again why, on the occasions when I get the opportunity to fully explain our position, I make it clear that we would provide special conditions for first-time buyers. We want to see people having easy access to that ladder of home ownership. So that we, almost irrespective of what we wanted to do on other forms of mortgages, we would want to see that sort of access eased for young first-time buyers.

BRIAN WALDEN:
But now you're starting to worry, as it were, the financier in me. I was very clear with you. I could see that old Gould was going to be absolutely ruthless on these mortgages. Now you are telling me that the people it would most affect . . . oh no, you're going to come up with a scheme to get them out of it. So who is it going to hit? What good's it going to do?

BRYAN GOULD:
Oh, this is very clear. The people who would be hit – but only in prospect, I mean they would be, they would be fully warned and would be fully alert to the change that had occurred in the interests of the national economy, and their interests as well – the people who would be affected by this, would be those who were trading up, those who over recent years – and again I say, I've done it myself – who buy, who move for one reason or another and find that because of asset inflation – the availability of this form of credit – that it is possible to buy a more expensive house and furthermore to obtain from a compliant building society or bank a little bit of money on top with which they can furnish the house, or buy a new car. Now it's that form of borrowing which has been so important, so crucial, to stoking inflation, and sucking in imports.

BRIAN WALDEN:
Yes, and of course it's also been crucial to the way the market operates. Am I saying, Bryan – and again I don't want to put words in your mouth, or exaggerate it – that you want a certain freezing of the housing market?

BRYAN GOULD:
Well, let's be quite clear what the Chancellor's objective is. The Chancellor, using an immensely crude weapon, a sledge-hammer, which not only affects the housing market, but everybody else including most importantly industry, he is prepared to bring about a fall in house prices. That's what he's . . . I think is his deliberate objective.

BRIAN WALDEN:
Sure, sure . . .

BRYAN GOULD:
. . . he's prepared to do that by hoiking up interest rates to whatever level is necessary . . .

BRIAN WALDEN:
And you'd freeze the market instead?

BRYAN GOULD:
. . . what we're saying is, not necessarily that the market should be frozen, but that the element of new borrowing which has stoked up that unacceptable degree of asset inflation, that that element should be reined back.

BRIAN WALDEN:
But it would inevitably – I said at the beginning, I'm not going to put words in your mouth – it wouldn't *freeze* the market, but by God it would make it pretty icy, wouldn't it Bryan?

BRYAN GOULD:
Well, I think those who are sitting on assets at present which are falling in value, and for which they have to pay in some cases nearly twice the mortgage repayments which they'd initially budgeted for, they would not recognise the market as being unfrozen at present. They would see the immense damage that's being done by the crudeness as I say of the sledge-hammer being applied to them. The effect of the measures that we describe would be much more specific, would be much more limited, but much more effective, because they would not be doing the damage to existing family budgets, nor would they be doing the damage to the ability of British industry to meet the level of demand which is currently being met from imports.

BRIAN WALDEN:
All right. Let me tell you one group they would be particularly effective against, a group that is always looking in fact to have a bigger house, and that is a growing family, a family with young children where more and more and more they need more rooms. Now your measures would hit them hard, wouldn't they?

BRYAN GOULD:
Well, in any broad acting economic measure, there will always be no doubt people who will be adversely affected, indeed that is the whole purpose, as the Chancellor will tell you with great authority, that is the whole purpose of any such movement to rein back an explosion in consumption and credit. Now of course we would make those specific provisions, as I've suggested, for first-time buyers. But if you're concerned about the problems of families wanting to move to larger accommodation, I can only

suggest you come to my constituency and talk to those hundreds if not thousands of families who are currently penalised by being locked into high-rise flats, and unable to move because there are no houses being built at all. That's the real problem, and if your heart bleeds as mine does for such people, I suggest that you concentrate on what's truly causing the damage, rather than on – what I suggest is a fairly marginal impact of the sort of necessary control over credit explosion that we're talking about.

BRIAN WALDEN:
Sure, but before we perhaps wind this session up, er . . . don't . . . it's always a joy to get a candid politician, don't spoil it. You admit, don't you, that it would have a deleterious aspect for people who have growing families. And you say: 'Well we've got to do something somewhere. They unfortunately are the people who would feel the pinch." That's the truth of it, isn't it?

BRYAN GOULD:
No, I'm not even sure that I would concede that. You see . . .

BRIAN WALDEN:
That's a pity, in which case . . .

BRYAN GOULD:
I'm sure you would love me . . .

BRIAN WALDEN:
Well we'll take it that you won't concede . . .

BRYAN GOULD:
Let me explain why because it's very important.

BRIAN WALDEN:
Time . . . all right, yes I will.

BRYAN GOULD:
I can do it in about two sentences. People generally in such a situation will buy and sell on the same market. If there is a slow-down, or even a standstill, in the rate at which house inflation proceeds, they will find that – what they lose in terms of being able to sell their own home and acquire a mortgage to buy a new one – largely offset by the fact that the price of that new house will be lower than it would have been if asset inflation had gone roaring on.

BRIAN WALDEN:
All right, well we, we've had a most interesting talk so far, of which I

think the two most important things that have come out, is that you *would* cut interest rates, and you would like to see them consistently moving down; that you fear recession from what is likely to happen on present policies; and that as far as credit controls are concerned what you would aim at is a limitation of the amount of money that goes towards new mortgages.

BRYAN GOULD:
That's right.

BRIAN WALDEN:
Now there's a lot more I want to talk to you about on this . . .

BRYAN GOULD:
I hope so.

BRIAN WALDEN:
. . . but for the moment we must take a break.

. . . .

BRIAN WALDEN:
Mr Gould, you have said that one of the things you would very much want to do, is to get inflation down. Now you haven't so far mentioned, I suppose because you haven't had the chance, one of the ways that the Labour Party thinks that that might be done, and that's by joining the Exchange Rate Mechanism of the European Monetary System. Now first of all, am I right, do you accept that this is a way that inflation might be brought down, and our exchange rate controlled?

BRYAN GOULD:
I think, all other things being equal, there's clearly a great deal to be said for exchange rate stability, and I think for that reason, we are right – and indeed John Smith and Gordon Brown are setting off almost as we speak on the tour of European . . .

BRIAN WALDEN:
Yes, they're touring aren't they . . . at Mr Kinnock's suggestion.

BRYAN GOULD:
. . . that's right, absolutely right, and that the – I think with the warm welcome awaiting them in Paris and Bonn and elsewhere they're right, so it seems to me, to explore the conditions on which a Labour Government – if we're not in the ERM by then – a Labour Government would feel able to take us in. I think that's absolutely clear. But in answer to your specific

question – do I see membership of the ERM as a means of getting on top of inflation? – I think that it would be helpful but not necessarily a guarantee. I think, I think we would be wrong to assume that somehow or another this was the answer to all our problems.

BRIAN WALDEN:
All right . . .

BRYAN GOULD:
Nor would I see membership as being some sort of hospital ward for an ailing pound.

BRIAN WALDEN:
All right, we might come back to that point. But you say that John Smith and Gordon Brown and all these splendid chaps, are going to get a warm reception in Bonn and Paris. I'll bet they are, because . . . let me ask you about this, you see. Labour is very cleverly putting the word around that it's a sort of enthusiast for joining the ERM, whereas old Thatcher isn't you see, she wants to stay out, she's got doubts and worries. But actually Labour's terms for going in are *much* tougher than the Government's, aren't they? For instance Labour wants a huge regional policy as part of it. It wants, in fact, a guarantee that the weaker currencies will be defended much more effectively than they are at the moment. And if that wasn't enough to upset them in Paris and Bonn, especially in Bonn I might add, Labour wants the whole purpose of the Exchange Rate Mechanism to be changed, so that it gives a priority to growth. Now be honest Mr Gould, these are much tougher terms than the Government's, aren't they?

BRYAN GOULD:
Well of course they're serious terms, they're not preconditions . . .

BRIAN WALDEN:
Tougher terms . . .

BRYAN GOULD:
. . . well let me come onto that in a moment. They're not preconditions that have just been selected at a whim, they are designed to meet very real concerns, not just I might say on behalf of the British economy, but in the interests of a properly functioning ERM. If we want to transform the European economy, then I think we cannot afford for example, to have the asymmetry which has meant that everybody has had to align on the German Mark, and in order to do so everybody has therefore had to deflate in order to prevent the German surplus from growing, and their deficits from similarly rising. So these . . . I use that – if we have time I'd be delighted to discuss the other preconditions as well – but I use that simply as an indication that we're serious, that these are preconditions

that matter, and I'm not suggesting for a moment that we're going to find them achieved overnight. But the big difference . . .

BRIAN WALDEN:
Or at all perhaps . . .

BRYAN GOULD:
. . . oh no, no, no, I don't agree with that at all. These are achievable conditions . . .

BRIAN WALDEN:
Well then let me put it . . .

BRYAN GOULD:
. . . and that's why John Smith and Gordon Brown are going. But let me just try to answer your question . . .

BRIAN WALDEN:
All right, I'll give you one more . . .

BRYAN GOULD:
. . . about the difference between our position and that of Mrs Thatcher.

BRIAN WALDEN:
Sure.

BRYAN GOULD:
Mrs Thatcher's conditions are in effect conditions entirely, or almost entirely, within her own control about inflation and so on. But she has no . . . no, she gives no indication of wanting to negotiate those conditions in any way. Her position is of standing with her face to the wall, facing the corner, saying I want nothing to do with this – we on the other hand are going to talk to our European colleagues, on the basis of an agenda which we are suggesting to them, which I think they will be very glad to discuss with us. We will see what progress we make. They are perfectly free to come back with counter-proposals, and indeed our negotiations will I think go much further than simply the conditions on which we might join the ERM. We should be getting in there with our own initiatives on how we then proceed to further stages towards what the Delors report deals with, but which does not . . . on which it does not necessarily say the last word.

BRIAN WALDEN:
All right Bryan, but as Mr McEnroe used to say, on this point you can't be serious. I mean the ERM is deflationary as you said yourself, and you've written about it, because they want it to be deflationary. You

don't really mean, do you, that the West Germans are going to say, "Terribly sorry, I mean we at the Bundesbank have misunderstood all of this for years, what we've got to go for now is growth," course they won't. When they come back with their counter-proposals, their counter-proposal will be: "Join the ERM like it is, sunshine, we're not going to change it." Isn't that so?

BRYAN GOULD:
Well. That may well be the case, I don't know . . .

BRIAN WALDEN:
Right, now will you join then, supposing they say that?

BRYAN GOULD:
No, wait a moment, wait a moment, I say it may well be the case. In the course of every negotiation people start from initial positions, which they then modify. But I think we have – and this is a marked difference, I might say, between the present day Labour Party and our, our predecessors – we have had already very useful discussions, principally with the SPD, in which we've already encountered a good deal of understanding, for the very obvious proposition, that some means needs to be found of dealing with the problem, and it is a problem, of the constant German surplus. Either the Germans have to run their economy faster, so that they provide a bigger market for other people's goods, so that the surplus is then eliminated in that way, or means have to be found through the regional policies or structural policies, of recycling that surplus so that it doesn't operate as a dead weight, if you like, in the European economy as a whole. Now the Germans understand that, the means by which we achieve that have yet to be decided, but that's what the negotiations are about, and it's the role of the ERM and our membership of it in achieving that, which is crucial to us and also very important to the Germans.

BRIAN WALDEN:
Well maybe the Germans in the Socialist Party understand all this. I don't know. I do know, and you know, that the Germans are absolutely obsessed with inflation. Notice that the Bundesbank – that's what caused old Lawson's difficulties – the Bundesbank proceeded to jerk the rate up by one per cent, when I'm sure you wouldn't have done. Come on Bryan, there is *no way* that they are going to say to you, "Yes, come in, tremendous growth, we don't care so much about inflation as we used to, we care so little about it, that we are prepared to defend the weaker currencies, we'll chuck our reserves in so that you can inflate in London." You don't seriously expect anything like that, so I want to ask you the crucial question . . .

BRYAN GOULD:
Ah no, no, no, don't, I can't let you get away with that.

BRIAN WALDEN:
All right, well you can answer both together.

BRYAN GOULD:
You put the proposition in the most tendentious possible way, which I certainly don't accept.

BRIAN WALDEN:
Answer both together. If the terms turn out to be keeping ERM very much like it is, would you, particularly in this present crisis, would you join it anyway?

BRYAN GOULD:
Well, as I say, I don't accept the tendentious way in which you put the proposition. We don't have to accept unlimited growth as it were, breakneck growth, no concern for inflation, that's not the deal at all. But what we do say is that we cannot as Europeans, we cannot construct jointly a European future for ourselves and everybody else, if it's all take-it-or-leave-it, this is what the Germans say and there's nothing further to be said. The whole purpose of negotiating, which we've done far too little of in the past, which Mrs Thatcher is still opposed to, she will have nothing to do with this, the whole purpose of negotiation is to draw the Germans and the French and the others into a proper debate of the sort that if we had more time we could indulge in ourselves.

BRIAN WALDEN:
We could, and we haven't and you rightly have stopped. So let me put this to you. You see, I have a certain scepticism about that reply, but we'd need a lot longer. A lot of people say there's a real difference between you and the Shadow Chancellor John Smith on this; that he is prepared to get in and that's it – without all this nonsense about growth and great regional development and all the rest of it – and that when he's in, admittedly at a more realistic parity, he nevertheless wants to keep sterling stable, whereas you don't. You're prepared to see a series of adjustments, namely devaluations, when we are in. Now is this true? Do you and John see it somewhat differently?

BRYAN GOULD:
I think, and I'm being as honest as I can be, I think people would be astonished at the degree to which John Smith and I agree on this issue. The preconditions . . .

BRIAN WALDEN:
Let's talk about where you don't . . .

BRYAN GOULD:
. . . the four preconditions after all were laid down by Neil Kinnock some years ago – a very good mark of the constancy and continuity of Labour policy on this as on other issues. John and I have, I think, possibly starting from somewhat different view . . . starting points, have progressively moved closer and closer together in support of that general position, to the extent – and here I don't know whether I'm speaking out of turn – but I don't . . .

BRIAN WALDEN:
I hope you are, come on let's have it, the truth, the truth . . .

BRYAN GOULD:
. . . I don't think I'm betraying any great confidences, but to the extent to which that, as John and Gordon set off on their European tour this afternoon, they do so having discussed the matter thoroughly with me and others, with my full blessing and with every wish for their success. And I have every expectation that they will arrive back, saying that they have had that warm welcome I mentioned, and that they've made significant progress. I don't expect that they'll be able to say, overnight we've achieved all the preconditions, because they are serious preconditions as you say.

BRIAN WALDEN:
That wouldn't necessarily cheer up the financial markets, and let me ask you this as a last . . .

BRYAN GOULD:
No, I think it would.

BRIAN WALDEN:
. . . well they'll think you see that you've pushed them towards devaluation, and unsound money and all that . . .

BRYAN GOULD:
No, no, I don't think so . . .

BRIAN WALDEN:
Let me ask you in general about the money . . .

BRYAN GOULD:
I'd like to be able to claim all sorts of great powers . . . but not in that respect.

BRIAN WALDEN:
What do you say to those people who would say, well now look, what with the minimum wage, and loosening the bonds on the trade unions, and he wants to cut interest rates, and in fact he's got other various inflationary things, what the City will read it for the Labour Party is *inflation* and that there'll be an enormous run on sterling directly you're elected. What's your quick answer to that?

BRYAN GOULD:
Well my quick answer to that is that it is not the Labour Party which is proposing to take risks with inflation. Those risks have been taken already, and we are living with the consequences now. I want to be quite clear, as John Smith was a week or so ago, that we intend to get that inflation rate down.

BRIAN WALDEN:
I must stop you there, thank you very much indeed Mr Gould. Thank you.

BRYAN GOULD:
Thank you.

22ND OCTOBER, 1989

BRIAN WALDEN INTERVIEWS ROY HATTERSLEY

BRIAN WALDEN:
As the Tories' problems grow, more and more people are thinking of voting Labour. The party has ditched its most unpopular policies but what has it put in their place? Does the new-look streamlined Labour Party actually stand for anything? The party's most prominent thinker is Roy Hattersley. Mr Hattersley, Labour's Deputy Leader, is with me here today.

Mr Hattersley, there is no doubt at all about the improvement in Labour's fortunes since the last election. You've shaken off a lot of the policies that were electorally damaging. The party gives the impression of being much more organised and much more disciplined. But quite a lot of people say: "Ah yes, that's all true but what does Labour actually stand for? We know what it's against, we're not so sure what it's for. What is its purpose, what's its overarching strategic aim?" And some people say: "Well, it's really degenerated into marketing. What Labour does is that it checks what the opinion polls say, what the public wants to hear, then it tells it to them without pressing its own convictions." Now, whether that's right or wrong it has led, as you know, to this claim that what the Labour Party ought to do is to formulate a 'big idea', a guiding principle which people could see was affecting its purpose, its policy, any disagreements that might occur. Is Labour going to have a big idea?

ROY HATTERSLEY:
I think we've got the big idea already. We're the first opposition, or at least the first Labour Opposition since 1918, to set out the principles on which our policy is based, and our programme will be based, and on which our government will act. And those principles are the extension of freedom through creating greater equality. It's the view of freedom which is the only practical view with meaning to most people out there: not the *theoretical* rights to do things which are only possible for a very small and privileged group, but actually providing more opportunities for the generality of men and women to take decisions about their own life, to make choices, to enjoy aspects of life which have never been possible before.

BRIAN WALDEN:
Let me just go through that with you to make sure that it is a big idea in the singular sense, because of course one of the things that happens in politics is that you have a series of things that cover different aspects and they tend to conflict with each other. You know, you want national standards but you want more local autonomy, you want more freedom but you also want more equality, and I notice that in that you did mention freedom and equality. Now which one of those is prior?

ROY HATTERSLEY:
The two things can't be separated. This is a long-standing argument between you and me, and between me and a lot of other people outside the Labour Party. I'm on the side of the philosopher John Rawls and, I think, all modern political philosophy now which says that freedom is meaningless without the capacity to put that freedom into operation. It's what Rawls calls 'agency' – the ability to do those things which a free society says you can do in theory. Let me give you the obvious example: Mrs Thatcher will say that this is a free country because you are able to buy aspects of health, you're able to buy a place in hospital, you're able to buy health for yourself and your family. Now, that may be one aspect of freedom, but it's not an aspect of freedom that means very much to the people who can't actually afford a hospital bed. For them, freedom is the right and the ability to get decent medical treatment when they want it, it's the agency that provides good health. It's that sort of freedom we're going to provide.

BRIAN WALDEN:
Well now, you see, that's interesting. I don't think we really do . . . we might disagree as to whether it's desirable but I don't think we definitionally disagree because, you see, what I want to put to you is this – there are all sorts of freedoms, there are all sorts of liberties that one can exercise. Some of them you would deplore as getting in the way of any progress towards equality. What you're really talking about is the extension of that sort of freedom that promotes greater equality.

ROY HATTERSLEY:
The sort of equality that promotes greater freedom. Let me give you an example, let me give you an example. When one of the defendants in the Guinness trial or the pre-trial came out of court, newspapers said to him "Do you enjoy being a millionnaire?" and not surprisingly he said that he did . . . and then being the newspapers that we have in Britain they said "Why do you enjoy being a millionnaire?" and he said "Because it makes me free, I've got so much money that nobody can tell me what to do". If we can spread it about a bit, there'll be more people who can't be pushed around.

BRIAN WALDEN:
All right, well then it becomes . . . if you're going to formulate it like that,

and you're perfectly entitled to, then it becomes absolutely clear that equality is really the big idea that you think Labour has . . .

ROY HATTERSLEY:
No, the big idea is equality and freedom, the big idea is the John Rawls idea that the two things can't be separated. Mrs Thatcher's great intellectual mistake, her great political heresy, has been asking the country to choose between more equality and more freedom. The two things can't be separated for the generality of people. She may have made this country more free, more libertarian for the people at the top of the income scale who can do more with their money . . .

BRIAN WALDEN:
Sure . . .

ROY HATTERSLEY:
She's depressed the amount of choice, the amount of ability to do what they want to do further down the income scale, in some ways obliterated it at the bottom. If you're a pensioner living on £46 a week you can choose virtually nothing.

BRIAN WALDEN:
All right, but you see, you did say to me, equality breeds freedom.

ROY HATTERSLEY:
Absolutely.

BRIAN WALDEN:
Giving equality a prior role in this.

ROY HATTERSLEY:
Well, giving it the role of agency, meaning the object is freedom. Equality is necessary to bring that object about. The Labour Party's Statement of Aims and Values – let me repeat, the first time for seventy years we've attempted to set down our principles – says the object of socialism is to create a more free society, to protect our liberties, to make more people have more choices, and equality is necessary, or more equality, not complete equality – that's impossible, in this life at least – but more equality is necessary to bring the greater freedom about. It's the means, not the end.

BRIAN WALDEN:
All right, I think that's absolutely clear. I think that equality is in fact the big idea – equality that leads to freedom, equality and freedoms. Let's now start examining it. For instance, if it is Labour's big idea, why doesn't Labour say more about it? Take Mr Kinnock's speech, for instance – lots

and lots of things in it but not the sort of stress you're giving me this morning about equality.

ROY HATTERSLEY:
Well, it does. Many of Mr Kinnock's speeches . . . I speak about it, I would say, with nauseatingly boring frequency. We talk about more money being spent on the Health Service, more money being spent on schools . . .

BRIAN WALDEN:
But that isn't equality.

ROY HATTERSLEY:
Of course it is, to provide . . .

BRIAN WALDEN:
Of course it isn't, that is spending more money on schools and the Health Service. That doesn't necessarily produce an equal society.

ROY HATTERSLEY:
One of the crucial ways of building a more equal society is to provide those public services which in the short term provide, for people in the middle or at the bottom of the income scale, facilities and opportunities which without those public services aren't available at the top. And what's more, a decent education service, a decent Health Service, is one of the ways of giving the children of this generation, the unborn children of this generation, a chance to emerge from their depression. If you look at the National Children's Bureau survey, "Birth to Seven" – what happened to every child born on one day for the first seven years of his life – you'll discover that what made this country unequal for the poor amongst those children was inadequate health care, inadequate pre-natal care, inadequate pre-school education, bad housing. If we can solve some of the social problems we make this country more equal.

BRIAN WALDEN:
A lot of that, of course, has always been said by the Labour Party, hasn't it?

ROY HATTERSLEY:
Of course, I mean, the basic principle, the basic principle has remained in my strand and stream of the Labour Party . . . oh, the radical wing of the Liberal Party at the turn of the century, T.H. Green and onwards.

BRIAN WALDEN:
All right, that I can understand and we've agreed that this is your idea of the big idea. In that case, what on earth has all the Mandelson – Peter Mandelson, Labour's Director of Publicity – what has all the Mandelson stuff, and all the various review stuff, and all the slogans, and the rose

been about? If Labour has always had the same basic idea, what was the need for all this great revision and rethink?

ROY HATTERSLEY:
Well, you can't sell a big idea in these days, in the days when people like you are so influential in taking political decisions – what you say and how you project us, the people you talk to – you can't sell the big idea without all the razzamatazz. In Mr Gladstone's time you didn't have to have this strange showbiz element to politics, these days you do. But take it from me, I'm second to none in my admiration for Peter Mandelson, but Peter Mandelson could not have worked his magic had there not been something to build on. He couldn't have made us the party which is double figure lead on the opinion poll if there hadn't been some policies based on a single idea that he could build this publicity around.

BRIAN WALDEN:
All right, you see, now I . . . I can see a lot of that, but I must put something to you about all this razzamatazz. See, take the slogan "Meet The Challenge, Make The Change". Why doesn't it say "Labour believes in equality"? The slogan's vacuous, it doesn't mean anything. If you're so keen on equality why don't you keep ramming this at people?

ROY HATTERSLEY:
We do keep ramming it at people, as I say, but we ram it at people by way of explanation and example rather than by philosophic discussion. Frankly, Brian, I don't want to undersell either you or me, but the interest in T.H. Green in 1900 and John Rawls in 1979 is a limited one as far as the British public is concerned. To get their ideas across, they have to be presented in a way which is easily recognisable and easily assimilable by a very wide audience, and that says: we'll be a better society if we spend more money on health care. That's a sort of equality.

BRIAN WALDEN:
Well, all right, Roy, I can see that. What I cannot see is how "Meet The Challenge, Make The Change" could possibly give anybody the idea that the Labour Party believed in equality. It positively obscures your message.

ROY HATTERSLEY:
It doesn't, it carries two very important ideas. One is the need for change in this society, and the other that the changes we want to make – and this is the concept of challenge – are not going to come about easily. We've matured through the period when we could say, and would dare to say, or risk saying: "It's all going to be easy, elect us and the sort of society you want and we want can come about quickly." We're telling people that we have to work together, people and politicians, to build a better society and there's going to be some difficulties ahead. That's what

challenge means and it's very important to get that idea into some people's minds.

BRIAN WALDEN:
All right, take your last Party Political Broadcast – although not yours personally – the Labour Party's last Party Political Broadcast. It was all about a rich yuppie.

ROY HATTERSLEY:
Yes.

BRIAN WALDEN:
And the difficulties and problems he had.

ROY HATTERSLEY:
Yes.

BRIAN WALDEN:
Now, that's not selling the message of equality, is it?

ROY HATTERSLEY:
Well, of course it is. Indeed, when you were asking me why we didn't do it, I was about to say to you what about the last Political Broadcast? Look at the last Political Broadcast: here is this man who thinks he can insulate himself against problems. He has a motor car with a chauffeur, he has an expensive house in the suburbs, he has private medical care, he sends his child to private school, he realises at the end of the programme that even with all this money living in an unequal society has penalties for him. And we were saying to that man, and men like him, we don't simply ask you to believe in equality out of compassion – important though that is – we ask you to believe in it because for even the rich and the powerful there are benefits in living in a fairer society in which things are more equally distributed. That was an equality broadcast, Brian.

BRIAN WALDEN:
Well, now, you tell me so, Roy, you tell me so . . . you won't be surprised if I have slight scepticism about that.

ROY HATTERSLEY:
Of course you have, otherwise we couldn't have a discussion about it.

BRIAN WALDEN:
Well of course . . . but for other reasons than having a discussion. You see I accept that the public may not in fact . . . let us say that up in Barnsley they speak of much else besides T.H. Green and John Rawls, I understand that. I understand that there has to be a certain simplicity of message, I

understand that as well. But you are not telling me that the way to pound it home to the British people that the Labour Party believes in equality, is to show the problems of someone who is very unequal . . .

ROY HATTERSLEY:
I think . . .

BRIAN WALDEN:
. . . why, why not in fact show all of the sort of problems in society where you could point to what you claim is the need for equality?

ROY HATTERSLEY:
I think we have pounded it home, and I think one of the reasons we're doing so well is we pound it home, and let me take some tangible examples. The world, this world, the world of Great Britain today is full of people who say: "We're going to do better out of the poll tax than we're doing out of rates. But we don't think that's fair and right. We, the rich, actually don't want to pay less while the poor pay more." We get these letters every day. You will read letters of that sort in *The Times*, that's the message of equality. We see letters from people who say: "We're sending our children to private schools but we know that, by the school in the next borough lacking resources, lacking teachers, needing rebuilding, we're going to live in a less well educated society and we're all going to suffer." That's the message of great equality. I think we've pounded it home by way of example, I think our success is built on that.

BRIAN WALDEN:
These people who write to you with their sons in private schools telling you that they are very worried about the state system, why don't you make it clear to them when you come along they'll be even more worried about the state system cause there aren't going to be any private schools?

ROY HATTERSLEY:
Well I don't believe that myself for a moment. I mean you must distinguish between what I believe and what is the Labour Party's policy.

BRIAN WALDEN:
Ah.

ROY HATTERSLEY:
I mean the Labour Party is not a party which is committed to abolishing the public schools. We're very clear about that.

BRIAN WALDEN:
But you're in favour of it, aren't you?

ROY HATTERSLEY:
I am personally in favour of it.

BRIAN WALDEN:
How can I be sure that these equalitarian views that you are giving me are actually the policy of the Labour Party?

ROY HATTERSLEY:
Because I've got a long record on your programme and others of saying: "This is my view and this is the Labour Party's view and either as Deputy Leader or spear-carrier on the back benches I will support what is the majority opinion." Remember defence, Brian. Remember when my view was not the Labour Party's view. Today my view is absolutely the Labour Par . . . oh to put it more modestly – the Labour Party's view is my view. But I always made it clear where the distinction lay, and that the primacy was with what party conference had decided. Party conference doesn't want to abolish the public schools.

BRIAN WALDEN:
OK, now it's interesting in a way that they don't. Let me link that to something else. Clear my mind of an unworthy suspicion that your political opponents of course will have – because they're in the business of having unworthy suspicions about you – but I think quite sincerely, and I suspect you do too, some doubtful people who are not hostile to Labour, but are doubtful about whether they're actually going to vote for it or not, may also have, and it's this: that yes, Roy Hattersley does believe in equality and most of the Labour Party believe in equality. But they read the polls with great care and, except in the very spacious sense that Mr Hattersley chooses to put it to Brian Walden, they've learned that it isn't a very equalitarian country at all. So the reason that their slogan is different, the reason that their propaganda concentrates on other things, is that they don't think equality is good enough to win the election. What would you say to that?

ROY HATTERSLEY:
I'd say they'd only believe that if they believe the thesis with which you started out the programme, and to which you've remained attached even though all my examples proved it wrong. What we have said for the last three years running up to the last election and immediately afterwards, is there are a number of specific policies where the disadvantaged must be helped and where the entire society is going to benefit through resources being concentrated on those things which in the long term bring equality. And that is the policy and that is what they'll get because with the Labour Party what you see is what you get.

BRIAN WALDEN:
Ah, well now you see just to . . . not I think that viewers would necessarily

think that this friendly discourse would in any way lead you to make an unsubstantiated charge against me, but just in case people think that you might have done, let me read you a couple of quotes. One is from Christopher Hitchens, very left-wing gentleman indeed – no Tory stooge he – and he says that: "Labour spends its time" – this was in the *London Review of Books* – "constructing anxious surveys to see how the electorate can be flattered and manipulated by changes of emphasis". And *The Spectator* said on your policy review: "A marketing man's manifesto, an up-to-the-minute catalogue of popular concerns." You see I'm not the only one – indeed I may not even necessarily agree with those statements – I'm putting it to you that that's what people feel. They feel that Labour doesn't want to talk about equality, it wants to talk about up-to-date popular concerns which often have nothing to do with equality.

ROY HATTERSLEY:
But those quotations Brian aren't from 'people' – that's what 'people' feel. That's what *The Spectator* feels.

BRIAN WALDEN:
Sure.

ROY HATTERSLEY:
I mean, a right-wing minority magazine which preaches free enterprise and can't pay its way in the world, that's not an opinion that's a prejudice, Brian.

BRIAN WALDEN:
All right and Mr Hitchens from the left?

ROY HATTERSLEY:
I'm not quite sure who Mr Hitchens is, but he's simply wrong.

BRIAN WALDEN:
Mr Christopher Hitchens is an old time socialist, great buddy of your former Prime Minister, Mr Jim Callaghan, who he used to talk to regularly.

ROY HATTERSLEY:
Oh the man who works for the *Daily Express*?

BRIAN WALDEN:
Yes he works for the *Daily Express* I think. Well is that so terrible? He didn't write it for the *Daily Express* he wrote it for the *London Review of Books*.

ROY HATTERSLEY:
Well it isn't, it isn't underlining his socialist credentials and it's one of his bits of biography you failed to mention. I mean, he's just wrong, whoever he is he's just wrong.

BRIAN WALDEN:
I see. So all the . . . any impression that anybody might get, whether it's *The Spectator* or the Liberal Democrats or Dr David Owen or Mr Hitchens or me or *The Spectator* or the *New Statesman*, that the Labour Party isn't putting enormous stress upon equality, and doesn't (sic), in fact, spend a lot of its time looking at poll evidence to see if it can cash in on things that are immediately worried about . . . we are all wrong, we're just not seeing the same world you're seeing.

ROY HATTERSLEY:
You are wholly wrong to think that that Statement of Aims and Values which you've written there, carried by Party Conference describing the principle I've tried to outline, you are wholly wrong if you don't think that's the basis of our policy. It was published and carried by Party Conference as the basis of our policy. You are wholly wrong if you think that we are . . . we believe that we can even possibly win the election on simply marketing. We're wrong . . . er . . . you're wrong because that's not possible and we are sensible enough to know that's not possible. Marketing is enormously important and no political party in the modern era can win without good marketing. But good marketing depends on good policies and a good idea. Every advertising man will tell you, you can't sell a rotten product, and we know that very well. And it's the product that Peter Mandelson has been able to build on, and his marketing would have been nothing without the material, without the product, there to back it up.

BRIAN WALDEN:
Well actually I think you've made it extremely clear. And I'm very grateful we . . . by this interesting little debate that we've had, and this question and answer, it is blindingly obvious now that the Labour Party does in fact believe in equality as you rightly say, and that you are not going to just market a rotten product, you're going to market the product that the Labour Party in a sense has always been marketing. I see you agree. Let me bring you back to that, you see. I'm not saying that all of socialism – a difficult word anyway often to define – can be captured by the . . . any phrases about equality, but certainly equality is one of the very distinctive features of socialism. Are you telling me in effect that contrary to what some people say the Labour Party hasn't changed? – it is still basically the party it used to be?

ROY HATTERSLEY:
The policies have clearly changed, they've changed with the times. But the principle is still . . .

BRIAN WALDEN:
The aim is the same?

ROY HATTERSLEY:
The aim, of course it's the same . . .

BRIAN WALDEN:
Socialism?

ROY HATTERSLEY:
. . . and you shouldn't be surprised by that. I mean if the Archbishop of Canterbury were sitting here, you wouldn't say to him: "Why are you still going on about the Sermon on the Mount, you've been going on about it for two thousand years and you're still not filling your churches?" You would say: "How does the Sermon on the Mount apply to modern circumstances?" And I'm sure the Archbishop of Canterbury would tell you. What I'm telling you is the principle, the great ideal, has remained but, inevitably and properly, the ideal has been applied to the world of 1989 and the next century rather than to 1918 or 1945 or 1964 when you and I fought on these principles.

BRIAN WALDEN:
Sure. As a matter of fact I'm not greatly surprised. But I think some people will be. Confusions have arisen. It's not your fault, you're very clear. This is socialism as was always understood at least by the Labour Party, isn't that so?

ROY HATTERSLEY:
You see . . .

BRIAN WALDEN:
You still believe in the same thing.

ROY HATTERSLEY:
. . . Well this is democratic socialism. There have been a number of heresies. I mean there was some crazy moment when some people said, socialism is nationalisation, socialism is the great state enterprise, socialism is the publicly owned monopoly running things out of London and telling people how to behave in Consett, County Durham, and in Newcastle and in South Wales. The idea that state control and state authority was socialism. That was a temporary heresy. The great principle of socialism has always been freedom and the great understanding of the principle of freedom is that it is meaningless unless you can exercise those rights. And that requires more equality.

BRIAN WALDEN:
So all this stuff that Labour has sold its principles, gone into the centre, now believes much the same as Dr David Owen, and all that, is in the Hattersley view, and indeed the Labour Party's view, nonsense. The

Labour Party believes in socialism – democratic socialism – as it always did.

ROY HATTERSLEY:
Of course.

BRIAN WALDEN:
Right, and so when the Tories go around . . .

ROY HATTERSLEY:
You say that as if you'd caught me out on something.

BRIAN WALDEN:
No, no, no not at all . . .

ROY HATTERSLEY:
I'm delighted to . . .

BRIAN WALDEN:
. . . not at all.

ROY HATTERSLEY:
. . . I'm delighted to proclaim it.

BRIAN WALDEN:
I know you are and I'm delighted to have you proclaim it. I'll tell you why – so when the Tories go around saying: "Don't be fooled they aren't in fact Liberals, they haven't given up all their old ideas, they're still socialists, they are still equalitarians" at least on that point the Tories are not telling lies, are they?

ROY HATTERSLEY:
The Tories are . . .

BRIAN WALDEN:
They are defining the difference between you.

ROY HATTERSLEY:
But that's not what the Tories will say. They won't go about saying the Labour Party is still a democratic socialist party because they know that democratic socialism is a very popular concept, not only in Britain but in Europe. I mean Mrs Thatcher is standing out against democratic socialism in the European community. She is standing out against French and German and Belgium democratic socialists. That's not their charge. Their charge would be about individual policies, they'll tell lies about individual policies not the truth about our principles.

BRIAN WALDEN:
Oh well . . . I . . . I must leap I suppose in between and say we shall see about that. But at least in turn . . . when they say this party has not changed anything like as substantially as people who don't follow these events very closely think it has. It is still the Labour Party, admittedly with some different policies, but with the same aims – the same aims for equality, the same belief in democratic socialism – in that respect it is telling the truth.

ROY HATTERSLEY:
If they were to say philosophically it believes in the same thing, they'd be right. But that's not what they're going to do, take it from me. Mr Baker's strong suit is not political philosophy. Mrs Thatcher is not one of nature's conceptual thinkers. They are not going to argue the next election campaign in terms of the ideology of the rival parties. They are going to argue it on rather squalid misinterpretations of individual policy items and I'll talk about those too if you'd like me to.

BRIAN WALDEN:
Well now, I'm interested to hear you say that. I think at least on the central thing we couldn't have it more clear and that no disagreement exists between us as what the Labour Party thinks it is about because they are . . .

ROY HATTERSLEY:
I've been reading transcripts of your programme in preparation. You always tell your guests you couldn't have it more clear, it's terribly deflating. I'd like to believe it was true but you say it every week.

BRIAN WALDEN:
Well you wouldn't want to feel . . . you wouldn't want to tell me you were very confused, would you?

ROY HATTERSLEY:
I wouldn't want to be left out.

BRIAN WALDEN:
You are very confused Mr Hattersley (*joking*) . . . no you are very clear. We've got it – democratic socialism – course you're right. It does have to be applied to specific policies and specific policy disagreements. I'd want to come on and test the big idea of equality against those, but for the moment we must take a break.

ROY HATTERSLEY:
Thank you very much.

. . . .

BRIAN WALDEN:
Mr Hattersley you've made it quite clear that equality is *the* big idea of the Labour Party, and you rightly said: "but of course they've got to apply this to policies." Now that's exactly what I want to do. I want to take one or two policies with you . . .

ROY HATTERSLEY:
Can I stop you for the third time?

BRIAN WALDEN:
Certainly.

ROY HATTERSLEY:
I hope I've made it clear that the big idea is more freedom which can only come from equality.

BRIAN WALDEN:
Certainly, I perhaps used a shortened and coded term of that multiple big idea.

ROY HATTERSLEY:
Don't want the *Sun* taking all the notes down to get T. H. Green and John Rawls wrong in their philosophical analysis.

BRIAN WALDEN:
No, no, I'm sure the *Sun* would be horrified to get T. H. Green wrong. Let us now switch to one issue that came up last week, actually on this very programme: the whole question of credit controls. What the Labour Party doesn't like, because few people do, is high interest rates, and it is suggested to the British people that there are alternatives by way of credit controls. Now in talking to me, Mr Bryan Gould made it quite clear that these controls wouldn't just apply to the fifteen per cent that goes on hire purchase, or credit cards, or that kind of thing, it would also apply – some measure of credit control – to the eighty-five per cent of consumer debt that goes on mortgages. And he also made it quite clear how that would apply. The young first-time borrower wouldn't be penalised, because there'd be a separate scheme for him. It would apply to those who traded up . . . those people for instance, like himself – because he said that he'd done it himself – who in fact had taken out a bigger mortgage because they wanted to move to bigger premises, and indeed to people with growing families, who have to move to bigger premises . . . that trading up would come under sterner credit controls. Well that's reasonable enough. John Smith however, Labour's Chancellor, at once implied that Mr Gould hadn't meant this at all, and that even if he had, he John Smith wasn't wearing it, that in fact what . . . all that Labour was saying was, that you couldn't take out a mortgage which you . . . part of which you then used

for purposes other than purchasing a house. Now which of these two propositions is Labour's actual policy?

ROY HATTERSLEY:
Well you really do misinterpret Bryan Gould. I've already said, without knowing this was going to come up, but I looked at the transcript from last week, and Bryan makes it absolutely clear that he's talking about a problem – it's a problem that the Chancellor's identified – which is people take out mortgages not to buy a bigger house alone, but people are extending their mortgage, second mortgage, to go on continental holidays, to buy motor cars to buy little boats to tow behind them. Now what he's saying – and he's right – this is a major problem of credit control, and it's a major contribution to the credit explosion that has caused us so much difficulty. It's a problem, but I don't think anybody has suggested we've got a pat solution to it, certainly not Bryan . . . and I see you're reading the transcript but I don't think you'll find an example of this sort of thing.

BRIAN WALDEN:
Well I'll read you what Mr Gould actually said. Mr Gould said: "The people who would be affected by this", that is the credit control he was suggesting, "the people who would be affected by this, would be those who were trading up."

ROY HATTERSLEY:
Yes.

BRIAN WALDEN:
Not buying motor cars; trading up – going from one premises to a bigger premises and taking out a mortgage on that.

ROY HATTERSLEY:
If that was a form of control that we could conceivably operate, but I tell you again . . .

BRIAN WALDEN:
Could you conceivably . . .

ROY HATTERSLEY:
. . . there's nothing in there, there's nothing in there which gives a scheme which can make that work, and we all know – the Chancellor has made exactly this speech – there is a problem here, we would like to solve it, but there are very substantial difficulties in doing it without penalising families who need a bigger house.

BRIAN WALDEN:
Now, earlier on you were not annoyed, in fact you were rather pleased,

but you chided me for saying how very clear you were. I now have to tell you you are slightly confusing me. I don't quite follow what you mean here. Bryan Gould said that the Labour Party's credit controls would extend to mortgages and he specifically said they would extend to trading up. Now is that the case, or is that not the case?

ROY HATTERSLEY:
No, the policy is what John Smith said – Shadow Chancellor and Chancellor in two years time – I don't believe Bryan said that. I believe . . .

BRIAN WALDEN:
He did say it, it's here in front . . .

ROY HATTERSLEY:
I believe, reading that text with the greatest care, as I told you I had before you raised this, that what he said, and I repeat: there is a problem in terms of credit explosion, of using houses as an asset which increases at a time of inflation in order to raise credit on other things. But both parties have said that's a problem. Neither party has got a solution on how to deal with it. And we haven't either. In any case, what John Smith said absolutely explicitly is there is no way in which we're going to penalise a family which wishes to buy a larger house, needs to buy a larger house, and wants to remortgage its smaller house, extend its mortgage to do so.

BRIAN WALDEN:
Well, it says here in the transcript that that's what Bryan did say. If you don't like the transcript, I'll give you another source. *The Independent*, not a Tory newspaper, in fact said exactly the same thing, that Bryan Gould was in favour of preventing people . . . at least, making it more difficult for people to trade up. However, however, let's leave that for a moment. John Smith says that in fact that isn't the case, so that isn't Labour's policy.

ROY HATTERSLEY:
Yes, John Smith couldn't have been more categoric.

BRIAN WALDEN:
Right, now again without blaming Bryan Gould in any way, what you're really saying in effect is that if Bryan Gould did say that there would in fact be penalties for people who traded up, if he did – and I say he *did* – then he was wrong and that isn't Labour's policy.

ROY HATTERSLEY:
Well Labour's policy is what John Smith said, so your treble hypothesis is, I suppose, right.

BRIAN WALDEN:
Ah . . . now, now you see, you see what that leads to . . . by the way I'm not going to pitch on about Bryan Gould, we . . . we both . . .

ROY HATTERSLEY:
I mean it is really like the Dead Sea Scrolls . . .

BRIAN WALDEN:
I know.

ROY HATTERSLEY:
. . . looking to see which word has been moved out and which has been moved in, but if you want to do it . . .

BRIAN WALDEN:
Oh, but it matters, and you know . . .

ROY HATTERSLEY:
I'm genially happy to pursue this line of argument . . .

BRIAN WALDEN:
Yes . . . I was actually there at the interview, and I heard him say it, and you know it matters. Nonetheless I'm not going to attack Bryan Gould, this sort of thing happens. What I want to get at is *why* it happens. Couldn't this be, you see, that the vagueness of the formulation that you gave me about Labour's big idea, means that there is no overarching principle? For instance, take equality. Where would it really apply here? You could argue: "Well of course you wouldn't discriminate against growing families who want to take a bigger mortgage, that would be inequalitarian." You could argue the opposite. You could argue: "Oh yes, you would, because the whole concept of private ownership of houses etc." You see what I'm getting at, Roy? There are problems in the Labour Party not having an overarching purpose that would mean that you didn't have to come on the week after Bryan Gould had made a statement, and contradict it.

ROY HATTERSLEY:
I think . . . I mean I understand the problem, and I think it's the problem of any political principle. If you take our opponents ten years ago, they were elected on the principle that the market solves our problems. Now you could, and no doubt have on these programmes, said to Mrs Thatcher or Nigel Lawson: "Doesn't look as if the market's solving this problem, what's more, Chancellor, it doesn't look even of wanting it to. Are you letting the market solve the problem of sterling? Is the market solving the problem of interest rates? Is the market solving the problem of the health service?" Any principle that a political party fights on is bound to have difficulties of application. And it certainly has difficulties of application

two years before you're actually in government. But the principle has, I think, been applied with unusual rigour to most of the policy.

BRIAN WALDEN:
All right, let's go back you say John Smith . . . er . . . and that's enough with Mr Gould . . . and I understand of course what you mean . . . let's now concentrate on John Smith. John Smith, you tell me, does state what the actual policy of the Labour party is, not the one that Mr Gould *thought* it was . . .

ROY HATTERSLEY:
That's what Shadow Chancellors are for.

BRIAN WALDEN:
Indeed, he tells you exactly what it is. But I have problems with that as well, you see. Would it work? It doesn't . . . you see, think of the reasons why it wouldn't. Supposing you did have restrictions on mortgages to prevent people buying motor cars and all the rest of it. The snag with that is it would leak into offshore sterling markets, wouldn't it? Or there'd be Deutschmark mortgages advertised in the *Evening Standard* – all kinds of peculiar things? Could it possibly have any effect at all without exchange controls?

ROY HATTERSLEY:
I've said before – I said ten minutes ago to you – that both parties have identified this as a problem, and neither party has been able to work a way, announce a way, in which the problem can be solved without unacceptable penalties. Whether we can or not, I don't know. But I said, before you even asked me this problem, the technicalities of operating it in that limited fashion are very formidable.

BRIAN WALDEN:
So we certainly are . . . let's . . . before I come onto that, let's get it quite clear, that we certainly . . . you . . . Labour's certainly not suggesting bringing exchange controls back?

ROY HATTERSLEY:
We're going to have some encouragement to bring British money back into Britain . . .

BRIAN WALDEN:
Sure.

ROY HATTERSLEY:
. . . for very good economic reasons. But if you remember when I was Shadow Chancellor what we had then was a tax incentive scheme. I mean we can . . . it's not physically possible to bring legal exchange controls back.

BRIAN WALDEN:
Ah . . . all right.

ROY HATTERSLEY:
I mean if John Smith, Chancellor, on the Friday after we're elected, announces there's going to be exchange controls that are legal, well people would turn the buttons and switch the knobs and the money will be out of the country before he's promulgated the order. It's not physically possible.

BRIAN WALDEN:
Sure, sure, we've at least got that clear, that in that sense you can't have exchange controls, but you can't have the old exchange controls back, you might try and do . . .

ROY HATTERSLEY:
You've got to have the prohibition, we think . . . you know the Bill was passed in two hours through the House of Commons in wartime when there wasn't any electronic control management.

BRIAN WALDEN:
That's right, and that makes all the difference.

ROY HATTERSLEY:
Absolutely.

BRIAN WALDEN:
But, but . . . now we can agree on that . . . let me now put something to you which I suppose you won't agree with, but a lot of people out there will. They will say: "Now hang on, hasn't the Labour Party been deceiving us? Because when Mr Lawson says we have got to have very high interest rates, credit controls won't work, the Labour Party has been very strongly urging the point: no, we could have lower interest rates because credit controls *will* work. Now the Deputy Leader of the Party says: well he doesn't know, he'll sort of do his best, but he's got really no guarantee that this would work at all."

ROY HATTERSLEY:
I've talked about one element in credit controls, and credit control is only one element of the alternative. You had an argument, I read that as well, with Bryan Gould last week, about deposit schemes.

BRIAN WALDEN:
Yes.

ROY HATTERSLEY:
And I noticed you took the simple free market argument, that if you had

a deposit scheme this reduced the amount of credit, or money available for credit, and that automatically put the rate up. John Smith, talking to the Governor of the Bank of France on Thursday, was told by the Governor, that thanks to the deposit scheme in France they'd been able to minimise their increases in interest rates as compared with those European countries that didn't have a deposit scheme. I mean that's one of the elements that *is* going to work.

BRIAN WALDEN:
Yes, there are two points there Roy: a) you go and have a look at the French savings ratio, and b) remember that France *has* exchange controls.

ROY HATTERSLEY:
Of a sort.

BRIAN WALDEN:
I mean you mustn't go around . . .

ROY HATTERSLEY:
Of a sort.

BRIAN WALDEN:
. . . just because a Frenchman tells you something, it isn't necessarily true.

ROY HATTERSLEY:
Exchange controls . . .

BRIAN WALDEN:
Many a girl has regretted that.

ROY HATTERSLEY:
That's a good joke, but a bad political point. I mean they have exchange controls of a sort, they have the most minimal exchange controls. They couldn't have anything very substantial and remain within the EEC.

BRIAN WALDEN:
But the French save more than we do . . .

ROY HATTERSLEY:
Yes.

BRIAN WALDEN:
. . . and they don't go so heavily into debt. Surely that's the key to it?

ROY HATTERSLEY:
I don't think it is for a moment. I mean I think that by having the banks

regulated in this way, a certain amount of control – not a very stiff control, but a control of banks – it did help to minimise the interest rate rise. And the other thing, you know Brian, we all know don't we, that the credit explosion, the consumption explosion, the worst figures on our balance of trade ever, the record interest rates, the appalling suffering of mortgage holders is very largely the result of the Chancellor twice putting too much money into consumption for tax-winning . . . for election-winning tax cuts. We are not going to do that either, and that's very important.

BRIAN WALDEN:
All right, now we've talked about credit controls. Let's talk about something else, which in a sense, longer term, may be more important – especially if your scepticism, which I share, about whether any of us really have got the answer to the particular problem of which credit control you would use . . . let me come to something that really is very important indeed. It's another difference, I think, between Bryan Gould and John Smith, though I'm not going to make much of it, in terms of a . . .

ROY HATTERSLEY:
No, no (*laughing*)

BRIAN WALDEN:
No, no . . . not in terms of a difference. I don't wish you to go into that aspect of it. But Bryan Gould very obviously takes these four conditions – that the Labour Party has laid down for joining the exchange rate mechanism of the European Monetary System – very seriously indeed. He also thinks that even if those conditions were fulfilled – and he takes them, as I think, as absolutes rather than negotiable – even if they were fulfilled, he would then, when he got in, expect to be able to have regular devaluations, because he thinks the British economy's uncompetitive, and can only be kept going like that. Now Smith, he's selling a completely different message. His message is that Labour's demands are negotiable – they're not absolutes, he'll sit and chat with them – there's a strong hint to some of the financial journalists that he won't fight too hard – at least he won't keep himself out of the exchange rate mechanism for the sake of the principles – and that once he gets in he wants to keep a fixed sterling rate, and there aren't going to be constant devaluations. Now, as the Deputy Leader and the leading philosopher of the Party, clear this one up for me, who's right there?

ROY HATTERSLEY:
Well on this one Neil Kinnock and the rest of us are all right and all say the same thing, because Neil made the statement . . . wrote a statement which became official policy – Bryan and John were party to it, and so was I – which talked about our enthusiasm for joining the mechanism if our four objectives could be met, and Bryan's a party to that like the rest of us . . .

BRIAN WALDEN:
Yes.

ROY HATTERSLEY:
. . . he was party to the discussion, didn't in my presence raise any of these questions that you've put to me this morning as his reservations. But let's not worry about that, let's talk about the actual policy.

BRIAN WALDEN:
Sure.

ROY HATTERSLEY:
There are the four objectives which must be met if we are to join. I've no doubt they can be met, and when they are met we'll be a more stable currency and a more prosperous country because we join. But the requirements are absolute. We want to go in, but we want to negotiate our way in. The question is, can we meet our objectives? My judgement is that we can.

BRIAN WALDEN:
But you see that leaves me in some doubt as to whether these are negotiable, or whether they are absolutes. But . . . let me take for instance perhaps the most important of them. There are at least . . . and we could argue about this I suppose . . . but I think the most important is the demand that the EMS gear itself to growth throughout Europe. Supposing the Germans and French say, especially the Germans: "Now sorry, we regard the exchange rate mechanism as being an absolutely crucial part of the fight against inflation. We're very worried about growth, I mean we'll . . . sure let's have growth if we can get it, but inflation comes first we are not signing anything that says that. You've got to drop that one." To get into the mechanism would you be prepared to drop it?

ROY HATTERSLEY:
But that's an absurd question if I may say so, to ask me . . . when you said let's take a more difficult one, I assumed we were going to deal with Reservation One about the swap arrangements . . .

BRIAN WALDEN:
Well yes those . . .

ROY HATTERSLEY:
. . . we'll come onto that no doubt in a minute. But the second obligation – to go for growth – the Delors report, which every other European country except us is going to adopt, talks about monetary union as being related to growth. We've got that already . . .

BRIAN WALDEN:
Oh . . . oh, come on Roy. Yes, *related* to growth. But you know Germans

always place inflation top of the list, and they will insist that John Smith does, and you do.

ROY HATTERSLEY:
But the Germans don't make this absurd theoretical distinction between inflation and growth.

BRIAN WALDEN:
Well . . . well try making it, because very frequently you can't have both you know.

ROY HATTERSLEY:
But Brian, I mean Brian . . . well what has bedevilled British economic policy for 30 years, including the party we were in together in '64, was the idea you had one economic objective and you pursued that to the exclusion of everything else. You remember we were always worried about the balance of payments and the sterling rate. The Germans have got enough sense to realise that growth, and managed growth, to a degree solves all the other problems. The Delors report will be German policy. It will be British policy after we're elected, but it isn't now.

BRIAN WALDEN:
Yes, yes, but I repeat again, of course we would all like high economic growth and very low inflation. Very frequently that isn't the choice available. The Germans have always put inflation first, and I'm afraid I must quote poor old Gould again. Bryan Gould is on the record as saying that the EMS is *the* most deflationary institution in the world, so he at least accepts what I'm saying.

ROY HATTERSLEY:
Sounds like one of Mrs Thatcher's economic advisers doesn't it. But it . . . I can only repeat . . .

BRIAN WALDEN:
It's Labour's Trade and Industry spokesman.

ROY HATTERSLEY:
. . . I mean I can only describe what the policy is. I told you of the statement – which we are all party to, Bryan no less than me – Neil's statement that we're all enthusiastic to join as long as the objectives could be achieved. I have no doubt they can be achieved, and the first objective – adequate swap arrangements – of course they have developed that in the EMS since our actual statement was made.

BRIAN WALDEN:
So, Labour in fact is adopting a very enthusiastic view towards a capitalist

Europe, even though you still believe in the old socialist principle of equality.

ROY HATTERSLEY:
Well I don't believe it is a capitalist Europe. I think that is a very jejune view. I mean Mrs Thatcher doesn't, your great hero Mrs Thatcher doesn't believe it either. Mrs Thatcher says, she's standing out against the socialism that is coming flooding in from Europe. She says the social charter, Delors, all that's coming out of the parliament, is socialism.

BRIAN WALDEN:
And you see it like that too?

ROY HATTERSLEY:
Oh, I think the social charter achieves and will achieve throughout Europe many of the things I want the Labour Party to achieve in Britain. One of the reasons that the EEC has been rehabilitated in the Labour Party mind is not that we've become more pro-EEC, the EEC has become more pro- socialism.

BRIAN WALDEN:
Okay, so if we summed Hattersley up, we would say he believes in the big idea of equality as being the centre of socialism, and he expects . . .

ROY HATTERSLEY:
Do I have to correct you again?

BRIAN WALDEN:
. . . and he expects . . . all right with freedom and all that . . . and he expects . . .

ROY HATTERSLEY:
Yes, freedom and all that, it's a big all that, Brian.

BRIAN WALDEN:
. . . he expects Europe to be the agency of it.

ROY HATTERSLEY:
Yes.

BRIAN WALDEN:
Yes, Europe the agency of socialism?

ROY HATTERSLEY:
Europe can be . . . I'm sorry I thought you said equality in there. Ask me the question again.

BRIAN WALDEN:
All right, Mr Hattersley I must stop you. Thank you very much indeed.

DARK SIDE OF A GREEN REVOLUTION

THE SUDDEN ARRIVAL of the Green Party in 1989 as a serious force on the British political scene took the experts by surprise. Everyone knew that the existing "third force" in British politics, the Social and Liberal Democrats as they then called themselves, and the Social Democratic Party, had alienated voters with their feuding. But few anticipated that in the European Election in June 1989 these parties would be beaten into fourth and fifth places in Britain while the Green Party swept into third place with fourteen per cent of the vote.

The new party attracted the attention of many people who did not normally follow politics, and its success became a talking point in all kinds of unlikely places. However, it was not readily appreciated just how different the Greens really were from all the more familiar parties. At first, people tended to assume that they believed much the same as everybody else, but were more concerned than most to tackle pollution and the other threats to the well-being of the planet, issues which were enjoying a lot of attention at the time. The notion of the sustainable society, in which activity was to be restricted to those forms judged consistent with ecological stability, passed many people by.

When some of the commentators began to understand what the Greens really believed, they became rather excited. From painting the Greens as naive innocents, they suddenly switched to treating them as dangerous maniacs. First it was suggested that if the Greens' approach were ever to be followed it would imprison many of the world's less developed peoples in poverty. Then it came to be suggested that, since the Greens put the health of the planet above that of their fellow human beings, if they were given the opportunity they would subjugate the latter in the interests of the former. They were presented as embryonic authoritarians, and dark allusions were made to the Nazis' fondness for the natural environment.

To the ordinary voter who had opted for the Greens largely as a protest against the existing parties, it was all increasingly puzzling. But as environmentalism gathered strength, and the established parties fell over each other in the rush to demonstrate their own green credentials, it became apparent that interest in the Green Party was not going to go away.

The Walden Interview clearly had to contribute such enlightenment as it could, and for once it would have to tackle the fundamentals of what a political party was about, rather than merely the latest twist in a story whose background could be assumed to be all too familiar to viewers. It would also, however, have to get to grips with the allegations of both impoverishment and authoritarianism, and give viewers some sense of the true price which would have to be paid for the benefits which the Green Party was hoping to deliver.

24TH SEPTEMBER, 1989

BRIAN WALDEN INTERVIEWS SARA PARKIN

BRIAN WALDEN:
This weekend, here at its conference in Wolverhampton, the Green Party is celebrating its breakthrough into the big time of British politics. In the recent Euro-elections it leapt to third place behind Labour and the Tories with fifteen per cent of the vote. Yet many people don't know what the Greens want to do. How radical are they, and how big a change do they want to make in the way we live our lives? Sara Parkin, a leading Green spokesperson, is here to tell me.

Mrs Parkin, anybody who listens to the Green Party or reads their manifesto or literature soon realises that the notion that's central to your vision is of a sustainable society, a society that in fact, in its extent and in the way it conducts its affairs, exists within the natural resources as we've got them, and the Green Party always contrasts that with the society we've got which isn't like that at all. Now, what I want to know is to get from here, the unsustainable society, to what you call the sustainable society, to move from one to the other, how substantial a change to our way of life do we need?

SARA PARKIN:
I think the change will be quite considerable, but it doesn't have to be a traumatic change. That's why the Green Party came into existence sixteen years ago, because we wanted to prepare for the inevitability of this, which you pointed out yourself. And we can take the step-by-step approach to move from the present society that we have – which consumes resources, is driven by the consumption of resources and energy, and the consequences of that is a lot of waste and pollution, amongst other things – we want to move to the sort of society which lives within the confines of the planet, the finite resources of the planet. And that you can call the unsustainable economy, if you like – linear, we like to classify it as linear: in one end you put the resources and the energy, and

out of the other end you have a product – it can be agricultural, it can be industrial – you also get waste and pollution and, as Mrs Thatcher pointed out, the richer the economy the more waste and pollution you get. But even the products become waste and pollution. So what the Greens are looking at is moving towards what we like to call a circular economy where you're looking at minimum input per unit of production, and you're looking at minimum output of waste and pollution with a maximum amount circulating, recycled round that circle.

BRIAN WALDEN:
Okay. Er . . . step-by-step movement, for a quite substantial degree of change to a different sort of society. How much time have we got? How quickly do we have to get on with all this?

SARA PARKIN:
I think we have to move very fast and I think that is one of the differences between the Green Party and all the others. The Green Party was founded sixteen years ago because we were worried about things like atmospheric pollution, because we were worried about the degradation of the planet's environment, but it's only now that people are really sitting up and taking notice. All the scientific reports have been coming in for some decades now, but politicians have not chosen to take them up. So I think the choices before us now are not whether we go green or not, but whether we go green in an orderly, in a planned way, or whether we are obliged to by some . . . some catastrophe.

BRIAN WALDEN:
I saw that one of your international affiliates, Worldwatch in Washington, was talking in terms of ten years, that if we hadn't got these things right by the start of the next century, there really was going to be disintegration. Would you agree with that?

SARA PARKIN:
Well, this is . . . they certainly do point this out and I in a way agree that we have to tackle the real problems that are facing the world today. We have to identify them, we have to recognise that they exist. Greens are often accused of being idealists but I think we're more realist, and we have to look at the fact that we're now . . . put so much carbon dioxide and other pollutants into the atmosphere that we've interfered with the weather patterns of the world. We have to look at the fact there is so much land degradation, soils being washed down rivers out to sea, that people are increasingly having to leave their homelands because it will no longer support them. We have to realise we've taken down so many forests that we are now looking at severe problems with the . . . not just the local environment where the forests are . . . but globally. We have to realise that pesticides which are used in Asia, in the South of Europe,

are now being found in the snows of the Arctic and the Antarctic, and so Worldwatch have actually said that we have ten years to turn things round, that we really have to address these problems urgently. And we in the Greens agree that. What we are concerned about is that we start immediately, we don't wait until things get even worse. You know we live in a sort of . . . what we like to call the post-mortem society where we wait until we see the dead bodies before we actually do anything, and politics at the moment, though Mrs Thatcher has indeed put these issues on the agenda a year ago, there has still been no sign of the sort of action that's needed.

BRIAN WALDEN:
I get the urgency in your comment. Let me be clear on one point, you see. After all let's think of how society got into what you regard – not everybody does but you regard – as an unsustainable condition. I suggest to you it is because basically the appetites have been materialistic; that in fact what we have been trying to do is to maximise product in order to create much more wealth. Do I take it that in moving towards what you call a sustainable society, that materialism would have to be tapered off quite considerably?

SARA PARKIN:
Well I think if you actually look historically at what happened, there's lots of theories about how we could have arrived here. I mean most of the other parties are blaming it on the last ten years of Mrs Thatcher. But you're quite right, it's taken a lot longer than ten years to get where we are today. I like to look upon it more as a series of errors that have been made in decisions. When we, as either individuals or collectively, have been faced with decisions, over the past few hundred years, we have gone for the simple option. And the simple option increasingly has been the option that can be counted in numbers, that can be fed into a computer. And so that we now actually run an economy that is dictated by . . . only by the things which can be counted in numbers and its successes measured only by things that can be counted in numbers, in money terms. And we've completely taken out of that, human beings – the actual well-being of you and I and everybody who lives in this country and indeed in the world. We're told that if our GNP is going up then we're doing better, that well-being of human beings has improved. But we now know that the spill in the Mersey of the oil recently, that and the cleaning up of it will put our GNP, that it'll . . .

BRIAN WALDEN:
So basically . . .

SARA PARKIN:
. . . it's illogical.

BRIAN WALDEN:
. . . basically you do agree with the logic of my question. You do want to switch the balance away from materialism, and you're not so worried about endlessly increasing the GNP?

SARA PARKIN:
I think it will. What we're looking at is measuring human well-being by indicators that are actually based on human beings. For example, health – Mrs Thatcher in her 'quality of life' speech actually boasted that more people were going through, being treated as in-patients in the health service. Now we would say that should be a negative indicator rather than a positive one. So human health, education, the conviviality of the environment in which we live, the number of species, the diversity of species that are sharing that with us – and so those are the sort of indicators that you can use to tell whether human well-being is increasing or not.

BRIAN WALDEN:
All right, I think everybody listening to that will have got a very clear insight into the general theoretical basis of the Green Party and the sort of society you're looking for. Let me now put to you some specific questions. Let's take a series of things that definitely harm the environment and let me ask you what you'd do about them. Let me start with motor cars – no doubt about the environmental damage of them – now what are you going to do about it? Are you going to ban them, or are you going to tax them much more highly, or what?

SARA PARKIN:
Well if you think . . . Green thinking is very much involved in not just considering the needs of one group of people against another, but also including the rights of other species, if you like, and the rights of future generations. So when we look at something like the motor car, we would consider it in that context and you also have to admit . . . .

BRIAN WALDEN:
And what would you do, Sara?

SARA PARKIN:
Well we're here in Wolverhampton which has a ring road put tightly round it which means it's very difficult for people to move around. Wolverhampton's planning has been totally devoted to the motor car. They say that in London now, you move round no more quickly than you used to do in the Middle Ages. So we're questioning if putting all our efforts into the transport policy for motor cars is correct. Not only that, but they are major . . . transport is a major pollutant of the carbon dioxide. So what we would do was shift all investment, or most investment, gradually step-by-step, so that people were moving around

by train, by canal, coastal shipping – we would, if you like, reassess the need to move things. How is it that cars are made all over the world and moved all over the world to different places, you know, why not make things nearer to home to meet people's needs?

BRIAN WALDEN:
Sure, but that makes it sound, you see, almost as if private cars would be a thing of the past. Now what about those inveterates who, for reasons of convenience I suppose, want to use a car – and it turns out that there are a hell of a lot of them? Now when you notice that, if you're in power, what do you do about it?

SARA PARKIN:
Well you see if the Greens were in power things would already be considerably different. I mean this is the danger of such hypothetical questions, you see. And I think you would find that people are already wanting to leave the motor car at home because it is getting increasingly difficult and unpleasant to drive around. There are a lot of complaints about pollution levels in cities. But people do not at the moment have a choice. They can't use a public transport system. It is difficult to use the trains and then perhaps be able to get a taxi or something at the other end. So what Greens would do, would quite simply, as any other government would do, would be make it easier for people to be able to move around without a motor car.

BRIAN WALDEN:
It's been tried in other countries you know. What tends to happen, Sara – now come on you know the world – what tends to happen is that we all want everybody else to leave their motor car at home so that we can conveniently use ours on a much less congested road. Supposing . . . and what always happens is you set these systems up and all the rest of it, but people still want to go on using their cars a hell of a lot . . . supposing you thought that that was pushing it to the point where pollution was becoming a really very serious hazard indeed, what would you do to stop the car owner doing that?

SARA PARKIN:
Well I pointed out you move . . . you would move the investment to make it easier for people to choose. I think you have to go back very much to fundamentals and realise that we are looking at major environmental problems. We're not just wanting to restrict the use of the motor car because we want to infringe the freedom of people to do things. I mean, we are not allowed to, there are rules so that we don't – we're not allowed to drive on the wrong side of the road, for example. Why should we be allowed to kill the planet . . . ?

BRIAN WALDEN:
All right . . .

SARA PARKIN:
. . . because that that is extremely important when you consider the details, you must consider them in the broader context. And some of my colleagues in other countries who actually are in government, either at state level or national level, or in local councils . . . Florence is a very good example: The Greens have actually done a local referendum and people have chosen to restrict traffic in the centre of Florence. And this has been a highly successful experiment.

BRIAN WALDEN:
What about the minority who didn't want to restrict traffic in the centre of Florence, what about their rights?

SARA PARKIN:
As I pointed out, there are rules and regulations in all societies – you have certain rights. You don't . . . you're not allowed to drive on the wrong side of the road because it's dangerous, you're not allowed to kill people. And so therefore, perhaps in the framework of the fact that we want to conserve a life-sustaining environment for future generations . . . also should be one of the regulations that guide us in our everyday lives.

BRIAN WALDEN:
All right, I get the idea that you want, by persuasion and occasional regulation, to reduce the usage of motor cars. Let's move to something else. What about air traffic? Now in my life-time, my heavens how that's increased – in the last thirty years prodigious increases – people now like wasps moving all over the planet they are. Now that can't be good, can it? What are you going to do about that?

SARA PARKIN:
Well I don't think it's good, it's certainly not good for the environment . . .

BRIAN WALDEN:
Exactly.

SARA PARKIN:
. . . and it's not supposed to be good for people either. And with the increase in air traffic you're now seeing an increase in disaster, and this is quite a good example. If you do more and more of these things you eventually have more and more disasters – at a smaller level of the air crashes themselves, but also the consumption of fossil fuels, the going down that road where you're doing a massive amount of consuming of resources. Now remember we're talking . . .

BRIAN WALDEN:
True.

SARA PARKIN:
. . . When Greens talk about consumption, . . . we're talking about natural resources and energy. And so we . . . the whole of society has taken the path where we ignore the consequences of consuming resources and energy – they're not accounted for. When you buy your plane ticket, you are not paying for the consequences of that consumption of resources . . .

BRIAN WALDEN:
So . . .

SARA PARKIN:
. . . and the pollution.

BRIAN WALDEN:
So should we have dearer plane tickets? Or should we not buy the plane ticket?

SARA PARKIN:
I think the . . . I think the Greens are for, as I said, making it easier for people to live ecologically. So therefore, we would be making the price right, making the price of whatever we do reflect its true consequences. You know we have externalised costs . . .

BRIAN WALDEN:
What about package holidays, Sara, are they out?

SARA PARKIN:
Well package holidays seem to have got into great trouble for a variety of reasons, because that is a sort of industrial tourism where people spend hours in misery at an airport, miserable flights, they arrive in concrete holiday camps which are increasingly miserable and, as you saw this summer, a lot of people are not going.

BRIAN WALDEN:
All right.

SARA PARKIN:
Now tourism, if you like, is about learning about other people, other places in a natural way, it's not – not an industry.

BRIAN WALDEN:
Well I see your views on air travel. Let's move on to something else now. I see that to a very considerable extent you want to dissociate the

economy of the country, the sustainable economy that you're moving to, from the present pattern of international trade. Now one of the things that that would mean – let me just check with you to make sure that it does mean it – is that our great propensity for bringing in Japanese hi-tech goods, Walkmans, Italian clothes all the rest of it, you would want some of that curbed, wouldn't you?

SARA PARKIN:
Well our relationship to the outside world is very important. You can't have a sustainable economy in Britain if you haven't got a sustainable world economy. There is no isolationism in anything Greens say, because one of the basic tenets is that everything is connected. I mean, we know from the problems of global warming and the accidents like Chernobyl that political boundaries don't really mean very much. It's one world, it is indeed one world. What we are looking at is creating self-reliant local economies, as self-reliant as possible. I mean, we are not against trade . . .

BRIAN WALDEN:
And that means no Jap Walkmans doesn't it?

SARA PARKIN:
Well this is a . . . why not make your Walkmans here? Why transport them? Because the Japanese Walkman that you buy doesn't reflect the true costs of all that has gone into . . .

BRIAN WALDEN:
And the same with clothes presumably, why not make the clothes here?

SARA PARKIN:
Exactly, because you could actually provide . . . this is where . . . it's security . . . I mean certainly the British are very much concerned with insurance against disaster. So if you're very dependent on the out . . . your needs being provided by long distance, then you're not very secure. So Greens are looking to the sort of economies that are self reliant, where most of our needs are supplied as near to where we need them as possible.

BRIAN WALDEN:
Of course there is one thing you would logically accept from this: necessarily – it's the reason international trade exists and the reason the problems have been created etcetera – necessarily, there would be somewhat less of these goods, wouldn't there? There would have to be?

SARA PARKIN:
There would certainly be, I mean it seems rather crazy that a jumper knitted in Shetland is sold in Italy whereas a jumper . . .

BRIAN WALDEN:
Sure.

SARA PARKIN:
. . . knitted in Italy is sold in Shetland. There is that rather ridiculous example of the biscuits that move up and down the motorway . . . because the cost of all that is not reflected in the product, and so the sort of trade barriers or tariffs that we would be talking about would be about the resources and the energy consumption. So that the nearer to where they were consumed, the cheaper the goods would be; which mean people could have the choice of actually paying more expensively for their Italian jumper, but more cheaply for something that was made close to home. And of course the implication for jobs, is tremendous.

BRIAN WALDEN:
Ah, I want to come on to jobs. But before I do let's get this absolutely clear, because some viewers . . . the unfamiliarity of some of the Green ideas . . . what this would mean is that there would be fewer goods around. The standard of living as currently conventionally measured would certainly fall, but the Green answer that I've seen to that, again and again, is: "Ah yes, but the value of life, the pace of life, the nature of life, would improve, and you mustn't keep judging standard of living by how much you consume. You would consume less but you'd be happier." Now that's more or less what you're saying, isn't it?

SARA PARKIN:
Well I think you hit on it there when you used the word, you know, 'value', because at the moment we are told what our standard of living is like by the use of the word 'price' – you know, price is everything. Greens are talking very much about a different set of values. I mean our values are . . . that new definitions of progress, progress towards a sustainable society, with the rights of future generations to an equally life-sustaining environment as we have. And so therefore what you value has to be really something that is going to contribute to that sustainable society. So that we're not trying to sort of say we're going to limit people's choices, we're trying to make it possible for people to choose in that new set of values where they are choosing not just for the here and now – the sort of live now pay later society – we want to make it possible for people to be able to choose now, so that they're taking into consideration the environment that they are going to pass on to their children.

BRIAN WALDEN:
Okay, now let's come onto a consequence of all this, which you mentioned yourself, and I'm glad you did, because I want to ask you about it: namely, jobs. Let's take . . . it's part of Green policy to fundamentally

change the nature of international trade, dissociate ourselves from the international banking system, and indeed gradually change the nature of domestic banking, making it purely local, and all that. Now there are about a million people involved in financial services in this country – and that's directly involved, let alone the spin-offs. Obviously you have thought through the consequences, have you Sara, of those people losing those jobs, which they undoubtedly will, won't they?

SARA PARKIN:
Well, I think the attitude to jobs . . . we prefer actually to talk about work, as opposed to jobs, and there is this sort of idea that there is this returning, as it were, to full employment. Now as you know yourself, full employment in this country took place for a very small period of time after the war, and it concerned only men between the ages of fifteen and sixty-five, so this idea of employment where you have a job and you meet all your needs by going out to work, and bringing the money home and buying them from somewhere else, is something that Greens want to shift, so that you're looking at the work people do. Now yes, we want to . . . we are not very happy about the financial institutions, because a very small percentage of their activity actually deals with the exchange . . . money exchanges that are involved with trade, that are involved with services. Most of it's just pure money transactions, and they are part of the whole money merry-go-round that is making . . . taking us towards the sort of unsustainable society that we're very worried about. And there is no reason why all those people who are employed at the moment in high international finance, cannot work at local finance, because our objectives with the local banks is that you and I, we do most of our banking in the High Street, and so do most of the people in this country, that's where we put our savings, that's where we borrow . . . now why not keep the money there, so that our savings are used to boost local economies, diverse local economies, small-scale businesses providing more jobs?

BRIAN WALDEN:
Well, now there are reasons, Sara, why that doesn't happen, but I don't want to go into that. What I want to go into is something quite different. This is – and I'm not saying it's wrong, I'm not saying it's right either – but this is by any measure a very radical step indeed, isn't it?

SARA PARKIN:
Well, this is possibly something that may be forced on us, because of the state of international finance, you have most of the money transactions are taking place . . . have got nothing to do with trade and services, as I said, it's also on the volcano of debt, so you have a very volatile and fragile situation. And as one economist pointed out about the EEC, you have *less* twelve countries making a market, you have a market that's pulling

twelve countries along by the nose. So this is a very, very fragile, and unsustainable situation. And so all we are talking about is avoiding the collapse of that, because we will be very vulnerable in this country in our own homes, if that collapses, and so will people in the poor countries.

BRIAN WALDEN:
Sure, but . . . but . . .

SARA PARKIN:
So we're seeking to build this self-reliance where we are able to provide more for ourselves nearer to home, because that's an insurance against international collapse.

BRIAN WALDEN:
Sure, but what I particularly want to stress is that all these people in unsustainable jobs better understand the radical nature of the change that's coming. For instance, I saw in your manifesto for a sustainable economy – your 1987 manifesto – you said this: "The self-employed will come into their own, cobblers, corner shop-keepers, smallholders, small farmers, craftsmen, and repairers of all kind." Now let's be quite clear, a lot of people out there are now in jobs that you intellectually don't regard as sustainable long term, and they better adjust themselves to the idea that they're going to move into some of these categories – cobblers, and smallholders etcetera. Now that's right isn't it?

SARA PARKIN:
Well, I actually live in France, where there has been less destruction of the cities than there has been in this country. And in the city that I live in, in a little small area, I can have most of my everyday needs met. I can have my fire-guard welded by the little welder's shop, because they haven't zoned the way we have here, I can do my shopping, I can have shoes – there's a very, very strong local community where I live, where the needs of the local community . . . there's commerce, there's business, it's all mixed up. Now there is nothing wrong with that. That is the sustainable society.

BRIAN WALDEN:
It's very different from the one we've got, isn't it?

SARA PARKIN:
But, but . . . what . . .

BRIAN WALDEN:
Some of these chaps in pinstripes better get themselves ready to be cobblers and all the rest of it.

SARA PARKIN:
But in a way Britain has been . . . more Mrs Thatcher, and previous governments . . . have felt that Britain's comparative advantage, if you like, in Europe and in the world, is in the financial and the insurance industry.

BRIAN WALDEN:
True, true.

SARA PARKIN:
But what happens if that fails, what happens to Britain? You know, it's the single cash crop economy, if you like. We've already experienced in Britain, in the North of England, when the steel mills closed down, when the car factories closed down, whole communities were dependent on one industry, so when they closed then the community was devastated. This is not secure and safe. The security is in the diverse economies at a much smaller scale.

BRIAN WALDEN:
All right, now I want to move on to another issue, but that has been all so fascinating and so important, I just must up-sum it, to say that you're making it clear that a lot of people, not just actually chaps in bowler hats and pinstripe suits, but a lot of people are currently working in a concentrated, undiversified economy, and that millions of them are going to have to be prepared to switch into a different sort of economy. Fair enough. Let me ask you something else. A lot of people won't realise, because they won't see that it's directly relevant to the sort of things they think of with the environment – you know, water and beaches and all the rest of it – that you also have very radical views on defence. Now I put it to you that you want to give up nuclear weapons, you want to come out of NATO – the North Atlantic Treaty Organisation – that you want to slash defence spending to the bone, that you're even prepared to allow people to withhold taxes if those taxes are going to be used to be spent on defence, and that you want trade unions in the armed forces. Now this is radical stuff, isn't it?

SARA PARKIN:
It's also sensible stuff. You've put it in very strong language, but it's quite sensible stuff, because this is the politics of the moment. Nuclear weapons are obsolete, both militarily and morally, there's absolutely no doubt about that, so why have them? We have also seen NATO – which is supposed to have been responsible for our defence – as soon as the 'enemy' makes a few steps towards peace, NATO has been left without a strategy. Yet we have invested a very, very large amount of money, a lot of very clever people, engineers, scientists, and military strategists, and yet we have been . . . it has been revealed to us that they have only one

strategy, and that is to make war. Now this is deeply worrying. And so the Greens say that what we need to be doing is taking into account what is happening now, the . . . what is a threat, you know, what *is* a threat? So NATO is already beginning to come apart, I mean, many people actually recognise that. What I see is a problem is that nobody is talking about what to put in its place. Now, what . . .

BRIAN WALDEN:
Well you do, to be fair to the Greens. Let me read you what you said Sara, you see, and let me ask you to explain how it would work. The Greens have faced this issue, and they . . . you say in that same *Manifesto for a Sustainable Economy*: "A realistic strategy of non-violent resistance to potential aggressors, this would be based on more self-sufficient communities, and the involvement of the majority of the population, who would be educated in methods of non-violent resistance to any invading or occupying power." Now how would that work?

SARA PARKIN:
Well this is the ideal of civil resistance, and it was used a greal deal, it has been used a great deal – the hedgehog – you're just so prickly that nobody would want to invade you. But you also have to think you know what are the threats that we are facing. That is our defence policy, to replace the aggressive, military – and expensive military – defence policy we have at the moment. Because we want to see – and this is already happening – that instead of arms being the subject of negotiation . . . but environmental defence initiatives, if you like. And I think this is where the SLD has made a tremendous mistake in that they said they would hang on to Trident, because I know by speaking to people in Europe, in West and East, that what they're interested in are combined heat and power stations fuelled by waste. You know, these are the international bargaining chips of the future. And so as long as we keep going back, as it were, holding onto the umbilical cord of the old, Cold War rhetoric, then we're ignoring the changes that are taking place, we're not taking advantages of the possibility of building peace on combined efforts to conserve the environment and stop its degradation and pollution.

BRIAN WALDEN:
All right, now this has been a fascinating session, because the degree of radicalism is high. Now it may be right, it may be wrong, but it's certainly very radical indeed, and that will carry some consequences with it. I'd like to come to those in a moment, because for now, we must take a break.

. . . .

BRIAN WALDEN:
Mrs Parkin what you are suggesting is radical, and it involves a lot of change, indeed some would say comprehensive change, I don't necessarily press it that far, but certainly a lot of change. Human beings being what they are, and British human beings in particular being what they are, lots of people don't like change. You do accept do you, that you're likely to encounter a considerable measure of resistance from some of the public to all this?

SARA PARKIN:
Well I think one of the most important points to make is that we don't have a choice about whether there will be change or not. The consequences of global warming have already started to be upon us. We're seeing hunger, famine, in the world, that's one of the consequences, and also the rise of water. So we are really in the next decade, in the next few decades, going to experience great change. What the Greens are saying is we can face up to it, we can be realistic about the problems we face, and we can prepare to handle them in an orderly way. And what we seek to do is to make it easy for ordinary people to do this. And I have the impression at the moment that quite a lot of ordinary people are beginning to understand the link between what they do in their everyday lives, and the global implications of it. I mean we live in one of the richest countries in the world, and it's . . . you can't get a clean glass of water, or chemical-free food and so on. And so there is obviously something wrong, we have all the scientific reports saying that there's something wrong. So change . . . we have a choice, the choice is not whether we change or not, the choice is whether we change in an orderly way or whether it is forced upon us.

BRIAN WALDEN:
Well now, let me ask you that very thing, you see. Let us suppose – and if ordinary people are becoming more and more aware of environmental problems it isn't impossible – let us suppose there was a Green Government, and you actually had to implement some of this. Now I put you back to the problem. If there was a Green Government of course a lot of people would have voted for you. What about those who haven't though, and who do not accept your analysis of the environment, and who do not show any disposition whatsoever to change their lifestyles in ways that are crucial, what would you do about them?

SARA PARKIN:
Well, you have a situation at the moment where you have a government that's been elected by a very . . . a minority of the population, and they are obliging us to do things that perhaps a lot of us would not want to do.

BRIAN WALDEN:
Would you?

SARA PARKIN:
So we would be very very enthusiastic about proportional representation and democracy, because it is absolutely crucial to what we do, that it is done with the full participation of a well-informed public – to say that, you know, sustainability and authoritarianism are incompatible, I mean history has shown that. And it's the crucial thing about what Greens are saying, is that we want a society that is sustainable, not just now, not just here in Britain, but for other countries in the world, and for future generations.

BRIAN WALDEN:
Sure, but you see, as you well know Sara, even PR doesn't get you round the problem of having to have a government. You've got a government, and you're sitting in it, and I come to you and say: "Look, it's fine, it's all right we're in government now, but it's absolutely terrible. To begin with there's air traffic all over the place, to begin with they're using their cars more than ever, there's more pollution than ever going on, the arms manufacturers have told us they haven't got the slightest interest in our proposals, the bankers are going on banking, it's a mess, we won't be able to sustain this economy, Sara, we've got to do something about it." What would you do?

SARA PARKIN:
But you are saying that we would be in a government where all this was still going on.

BRIAN WALDEN:
Sure, of course . . .

SARA PARKIN:
I would consider that when if we were in a government things would be considerably different already.

BRIAN WALDEN:
Why?

SARA PARKIN:
Because there will . . . either we will be further down the road to the problems, and certainly we would have the support of people. And we have got a series of measures to make this step-by-step change from what I said was the linear economy to the sustainable one. And in areas, this is already happening, you're seeing more local businesses being set up, you are seeing the banks really deeply worried about their problems of debt.

BRIAN WALDEN:
But Sara, if it was all going to happen anyway, there'd be no reason to have the Green Party. I'm putting it to you, that you are a political party, that you want to secure power, because you believe that only you have the correct analysis of how in fact the environment can be saved. So now I'm saying, all right you've won, you're there, you've got it. And I'm coming to tell you that there are a lot of recalcitrant people who won't do what we want them to. What are you going to do about them?

SARA PARKIN:
This is such a crazy hypothetical question.

BRIAN WALDEN:
Why?

SARA PARKIN:
Because what the Greens would do if we were in government is . . . I mean this is beginning to happen already. Mrs Thatcher has very much gone for the eco-labelling, so this is informing people, so that in their everyday lives, they can make a choice. At the moment . . .

BRIAN WALDEN:
But they don't want to . . . they don't listen.

SARA PARKIN:
But people don't know the information, and you must admit this yourself, that at the moment when people make a choice on what they buy in the supermarket, whether they drive their car or not, it is done on limited information. Absolutely crucial is that people have the information to make those choices. And I think once you have that information, that helps a great deal. Now if you back that up by strategic planning, which would be clear steps on how we move from one sort of economy to a sustainable society . . .

BRIAN WALDEN:
Backed by what, Sara, compulsion?

SARA PARKIN:
No, with . . .

BRIAN WALDEN:
Persuasion again?

SARA PARKIN:
. . . active fiscal policy . . .

BRIAN WALDEN:
Tariffs?

SARA PARKIN:
. . . high standards . . .

BRIAN WALDEN:
Tariffs, let's be clear on active fiscal policy, tariffs, tariffs . . .?

SARA PARKIN:
. . . and public investment in the right direction. In all the things that I said earlier, we could do less moving from one to the other, this would be done by explaining things to people. Because at the moment we have a secret government, there are not (sic) access to the way decisions are being made, many things are happening without consultation of the public, so therefore there is resistance. And we believe that if people understand fully that what the Greens are talking about is the future, children, we've got grand . . . future generations must have a life-sustaining environment. And if you are actually framing everything you do in the understanding that the new shift of values, if it was away from the I, the me, the live now, the pay later, this sort of credit card society, which we're now getting back, externalising the costs, it's the environment pays, future generation pays – now if people understand that, if we have a very democratic society, fully informed society, then we can take the step-by-step approach. We would not be in government in the same way Mrs Thatcher's in government, we would be in government with a proper democracy.

BRIAN WALDEN:
Well we'll see. I want to put, I must press you on this Sara, because it's not clear to me whether you think you're in the business of supplying information, or whether you're in serious politics. I have never known a major politician who didn't think that if only he could get his point of view clearly over to the public, there wouldn't be a problem, and I can tell you – you're laughing, you know it, they all say that – it isn't true. You would get it over to the public and a lot of them wouldn't take any notice. And in that list of things that you told me that you would do about it, you mentioned tariffs, now they're coercive, aren't they? If you put tariffs on, that means that people can't buy some of the things at the same price that they used to. And if you put tariffs on exports, which is one of your suggestions, that means in fact that people can't send goods out in the way they used to. Face it, you can't dodge the coercion issue, can you? You're going to have to use a certain amount of compulsion however much information you supply, aren't you?

SARA PARKIN:
We are not going to use the sort of coercion in the way that you are implying that we would. We would use the same fiscal incentives and disincentives that any government would use to encourage people to move in a certain direction. We're actually trying to make it easier for people to live their lives in a sustainable way. We have already a lot of evidence – not just from the opinion polls for our support, but the underlying, more deeper polls – that we're seeing a shift in values. Now it depends whether you go on arguing what we do in the same rhetoric, in the same framework of old politics, or whether you really start thinking that the whole set of values, the whole game plan has shifted, because we're no longer dealing with the interests of one group of people against another, but we're also dealing with the interests of future generations. And that shifts the whole way of looking at problems. And so . . .

BRIAN WALDEN:
I suspect – can I come in here, because there's another thing I want to ask you – I suspect that some viewers watching this will say, Mrs Parkin is a good woman, well intentioned and all that – they'll be slightly patronising, which I'm not – but she's rather naive. Now I don't think you're rather naive at all. I think you're more cunning than you look. Let me give you an example. Your Party started this week saying that within sixty years, there'd got to be a twenty-five per cent reduction of the population. I notice you're not saying that now. Why? Because you're afraid of this coercion point, aren't you? You're getting chicken feet about this. You're afraid that you will be portrayed as people who will coerce. So gradually you're trying to ditch the coercive elements in your policy, which is not naivety at all, very clever politics, isn't it?

SARA PARKIN:
No, I think you've quite misinterpreted that whole business – the press picked up very much on that. What we're talking about is the carrying capacity of the planet.

BRIAN WALDEN:
Sure.

SARA PARKIN:
Now, we live in a rich country, and we're part of the very twenty per cent of the world that consumes eighty per cent of the resources. So when you're looking at a carrying capacity of any part of the globe, you're looking to the number of people that it can support sustainably.

BRIAN WALDEN:
Sure.

SARA PARKIN:
If that breaks down, people die . . .

BRIAN WALDEN:
I knew all that, you had a policy on that, why have you changed it?

SARA PARKIN:
No, no what we have done is taken out the figures because people . . .

BRIAN WALDEN:
Why?

SARA PARKIN:
. . . because people like you will say that it is coercive. We were talking about the sort of numbers that could be carried by Great Britain, in the same way that they look at other countries. Now this has not been done, nobody has actually examined the carrying capacity of Europe, or any of the European countries. We don't have to, because we can import lots of our raw materials, lots of our basic food stuffs from the rest of the world. But when we can't, when we can no longer use the resources of the rest of the world, because their population's growing, because of the global warming, which is causing more famine, more desertification, and raising water, you know, then you are very much going to have to face up to the fact that if we wish to lighten our load on the planet, then one of the things to do is look at the absolute numbers of human beings. And that's . . .

BRIAN WALDEN:
I understand it, but Sara let me put this to you, you see by taking the target figures out, you haven't abolished the problem. Supposing you discover that instead of shrinking down the population starts to come up, it's another one of these, what are you going to do about it problems. What will you do about it?

SARA PARKIN:
It was never a target figure. It was a 'say', we would, you know what the carrying capacity of Britain might be would be say, between . . . nobody knows it but it's very important . . .

BRIAN WALDEN:
Sure, but certainly a lot less than it is at the moment.

SARA PARKIN:
. . . and I also would, and I think this is perhaps the point to let you know that I was a nurse, and I also worked for a long time in family planning, and in sex education and relationship counselling. And in my

work in this country, I discovered a great number of people had very limited information about their own bodies, about sex, and about the consequences.

BRIAN WALDEN:
So it's persuasion and information.

SARA PARKIN:
A lot of people who would like access to family planning materials can either not get it, or they find the facilities distasteful. So all you are doing is making people aware of the problem, and you are offering the means by which they can make a personal choice in the global context of the new politics of the future.

BRIAN WALDEN:
Sure. Let me ask you this, you see. I'm intrigued by the way this latter part of the discussion has gone. A lot of people watching will say: "well I agree with a lot of what she says, but every time she's offered a difficult problem she says well she wouldn't coerce etcetera." Why didn't you stay as a pressure group, instead of getting into the game called politics, where you have to coerce, and you have to have compulsion and you have to have laws. Why didn't you stay as a pressure group?

SARA PARKIN:
Well I used to belong to a pressure groups, and the reason I joined the Green Party in 1977, was because I understood that the only pressure respected by . . .

BRIAN WALDEN:
Regrettably Mrs Parkin, we've run out of time. Thank you very much indeed, I'm so sorry.